POLITICO-ECONOMIC IDEAS OF MAHATMA GANDHI

Gandhian Studies and Peace Research Series

1. Gandhian Model of Development and World Peace, **R.P. Misra**
   Conflict Resolution Through Non-Violence: Role of the Universities (in two Vols.), **K.D. Gangrade** and **R.P. Misra (eds.)**
2. Vol. 1: Science and Ethics, **K.D. Gangrade** and **R.P. Misra**
3. Vol. 2: Development without Destruction, **K.D. Gangrade** and **R.P. Misra**
4. The Social Philosophy of Mahatma Gandhi, **K.S. Bharathi**
5. Gandhian Humanism, **Mohit Chakrabarti**
6. Gandhian Holistic Economics, **Shashi Prabha Sharma**
7. Gandhian Spiritualism: A Quest for Essence of Excellence, **Mohit Chakrabarti**
8. Gandhian Perspective on Population and Development, **A.K. Sharma**
9. Thoughts of Gandhi and Vinoba: A Comparative Study, **K.S. Bharathi**
10. Economic Philosophy of Mahatma Gandhi, **Shanti Swarup Gupta**
11. Political Thought of Mahatma Gandhi (The), **K.S. Bharati**
12. Gandhi and 21st Century, **Janardhan Pandey (ed.)**
13. Gandhian Philosophy of the Spinning Wheel, **Mohit Chakraborti**
14. Gandhian Satyagraha: An Analytical and Critical Approach, **Ajay Shanker Rai**
15. Gandhi and His Religion, **(Lt. Col.) P. A. Raju**
16. महात्मा गाँधी विचार वीथिका, **एस. पी. अग्रवाल**
17. Poverty of Gandhian Philosophy, **Himansu Roy**
18. Right to Equality in the Indian Constitution: A Gandhian Perspective, **Shashi Nath Saraswati**
19. Meditations on Gandhi: A Ravindra Varma Festschrift, **M.P. Mathai, M.S. John** and **Siby K. Joseph (eds.)**
20. Politico-Economic Ideas of Mahatma Gandhi: Their Relevence in the Present-Day, **Sukhendu Mazumdar**
21. Moral Lessons from Gandhi's Autobiography and Other Essays, **K.D. Gangrade**

About the Author

Dr. Sukhendu Mazumder, (M.A., Ph.D) a well-known Gandhian scholar and social scientist, presently works as a civilian instructor in a paramilitary organisation. Earlier, he worked as a Headmaster of a High School (in Mon district in Nagaland) and Principal of a college (at Dimapur in Nagaland). Dr. Mazumdar has over half a dozen published research papers to his credit. Also, he has attended many seminars and conferences.

Gandhian Studies and Peace Research Series – 20

POLITICO-ECONOMIC IDEAS OF MAHATMA GANDHI

Their Relevance in the Present-Day

SUKHENDU MAZUMDER

CONCEPT PUBLISHING COMPANY, NEW DELHI-110059

Cataloging in Publication Data—DK
Courtesy: D.K. Agencies (P) Ltd. <docinfo@dkagencies.com>

Mazumder, Sukhendu, 1951-
Politico-economic ideas of Mahatma Gandhi, their relevance in the present-day / Sukhendu Mazumder,
p. cm.
(Gandhian studies and peace research series ; 20)
Includes bibliographical references (p.)
Includes index.
ISBN 81-8069-109-8

1. Gandhi, Mahatma, 1869-1948—Political and social views. 2. Gandhi, Mahatma, 1869-1948—Views on economic development. 3. India—Politics and government. 4. India—Economic conditions. I. Title. II. Series: Gandhian studies and peace research series ; 20.

DDC 954.035 21

ISBN 81-8069-109-8

First Published 2004

Published and Printed by
Ashok Kumar Mittal
Concept Publishing Company
A/15-16, Commercial Block, Mohan Garden
New Delhi-110059 (INDIA)

Phones: 25351460, 25351794
Fax: 091-11-25357103
E-mail: publishing@conceptpub.com

Dedicated

to

SRI SRI THAKUR ANUKUL CHANDRA

Founder of SATSANG (PABNA)

Preface

It has indeed become a very controversial issue whether the Gandhian concepts can be put to use on the Economic and Political fore. Yet, things seem to be quite misleading, complex and amusing too, when for the sake of political gains,—the Mahatma's thoughts are uttered with precision. But, what is very sadly missed, is,—the way Gandhiji wanted things to move can still be practised with success. The great soul, perhaps, went deep into the problems and studied the basic nature where it really mattered. And hence, his words though simple and lucid, were at the same time so deep that it was not possible for anybody to reach that height. It was not possible either to excel him in his lifetime or even after 40 years no one can claim to have done better. "To try to interpret Gandhiji is as complex a task as to interpret Hinduism. Just as in the latter case, one can quote scriptures without end and yet miss the essence, so in his case one can pile quotation on quotation and miss the man."* So there is no denying the fact that if we dedicate to the nation's upliftment in all aspects of the term, 'it' is still in vogue and can safely be launched and practised in both the fronts — political and economic — with amazing success. Though resources are limited and one cannot penetrate this multidimensional ideology, the efforts are put with the belief that 'Truth' prevails.

I am thankful to my supervisor Dr. K.R.P. Singh, M.A., Ph.D., Reader, Bhagalpur University, for his guidance in my

* Sunday Review, *The Times of India,* by Girilal Jain, Oct. 3, 1982, p. 1.

research work. I acknowledge my debt to Dr. S.N. Thakur, M.A. (Pat), M.A. (Michigan), Ph.D., Ex-head of the University Department of Economics, Bhagalpur University, without whom the work was not at all possible. He encouraged me from beginning to the end. Dr. Ramjee Singh, M.A., Ph.D., D.Litt., Ex-M.P., the Head of the University Department of Gandhian Thought, Bhagalpur University, has also helped me a lot.

I ascribe the completion and success to all concerned and humbly accept my inability, if any.

Sukhendu Mazumder

167/B, Dakshinpara Road,
Kolkata-700 028

Contents

1

Introduction

India won freedom on 15th August, 1947. The power of non-violence proved to be the most powerful method of breaking all the barriers that stood in the way. It was a miracle before the world. The world had never witnessed such power before : Yet, it looked so simple and easy that everybody could understand, but it reeled the heads of most intellectuals of the world !

Hence, a humble attempt is made to study the great figure which influenced the every nook and corner of the country, every heart from the grassroots to the top. To quote Larry Collins and Dominique Lapierre from *Freedom at Midnight,* — To a century fraught with violence, Gandhi offered an alternative—non-violence and civil disobedience. In Churchill's famous phrase, a "half-naked fakir" Gandhi crisscrossed his nation on foot and in third-class railway cars to stress his identity with the impoverished masses. He took tea at Buckingham Palace with King Emperor, dressed in the homespun cotton sheet that was his uniform, and practised a life of spartan simplicity. The symbol of his challenge to the Age of Imperialism was the primitive wooden spinning wheel on which he laboured religiously everyday."[1]

Moreover, Gandhiji was never an economist nor a politician in the academic sense or the traditional sense of the term. He never wove his thoughts under a particular system, nor did he try to give shape to them accordingly. But he is the only one in the world to bring Economics, Politics, Ethics etc. close and available to the mass. Though one can say that, "Gandhi was not an economist."[2] Or, the same can be said in other branches of knowledges too. So the task of blending his ideas is difficult and requires much patience to apply the blend to suit or to reject in the relevance of present-day India.

The Mahatma, in fact, remained so powerful an embodiment of truth and non-violence and yet so practical a person that sometimes he keeps us guessing. In the words of Larry Collins and Dominique Lapierre, "The Mahatma had, indeed, been a difficult person for the British to deal with. Truth, to Gandhi, was ultimate reality. Gandhiji's truth, however, had two faces, the absolute and the relative. Man, as long as he was in the flesh, had only fleeting intimations of absolute truth. He had to deal with relative truth in his daily existence. Gandhi liked to employ a parable to illustrate the difference between his two truths. Put your left hand in a bowl of ice-cold water, then in a bowl of luke-warm water, he would say. The luke-warm water feels hot. Then put the right hand in a bowl of hot water and into the same bowl of luke-warm water. Now the luke-warm water feels cold; yet its temperature, is constant. The absolute truth is the water's constant temperature, he would observe, but the relative truth, perceived by the human hand, varied. As that parable indicated, Gandhi's relative truth was not a rigid thing. It could vary as his perceptions of a problem changed. That made him flexible but it also, to his British interlocutors, sometimes made him appear a two-faced, cunning Asiatic. Even of his disciples once explained to him in exasperation, 'Gandhiji, I don't understand you. How can you say one thing last week, and something quite different this week?' 'Ah', Gandhi replied, 'because I have learned something since last week.' "[3] So this clearly shows to what extent a man may be practical. He was never so rigid, as is held so far. He always welcomed anything modern in the greater interest of the masses. It is still felt in many corners, that he opposed the use of machineries in favour of home-industries and other labour-intensive occupations. But, what he really opposed was not the use of machinery, he wanted the labour to be employed and minimum requirements of the labour to be fulfilled. He did not oppose even the large machineries, if they served the cause of the masses. It would be utter folly to judge the Mahatma on the pretext that he did not see anything beyond the wheels of *Charkha.* Rather, he opted the most suited weapon to fight the problem of that time. He was ever ready to change and accommodate things as called for. He was, in brief, much more aware of the sufferings of the masses than anybody of the world. He visited every part of the country and had made a thorough study of the conditions of masses. He knew how to solve them and how to bring peace and harmony. That is why he always stressed physical labour and co-operation with non-violence and above all the 'Truth'. His truth was his God. He did see no difference between the truth and the God.

His *Satyagraha* too was not the weapon of the weak. To quote Prof. R.R. Diwakar in '*Satyagraha',*—"The most important aspects of Satyagraha are two. It is a way of life and a weapon for fighting injustice—social, economic and political.

Satyagraha as a way of life means the total acceptance of its philosophy and a ceaseless endeavour to live up to that ideal. It is as old as the hills and yet, as embodied in Gandhiji's life, it is as fresh as the green grass."[4]

So, we see, Gandhiji in total is as big as the Himalayas, as high as the sky and hence, we require that much of ability to study and apply his subtle but accurate principles and policies, which at times seem quite a difficult task, if not impossible. Yet, in spite of the various shortcomings and many a problems, efforts have been made to study and present the Mahatma by using the available matters and consulting eminent scholars with Gandhian outlook.

Gandhiji's ideas, at times, appear utopian and impractical to modern economists, other social scientists, politicians and statesmen. The reason is that Gandhiji preached what he himself practised in life. But in modern times the above mentioned galaxy of people preach what they never practise themselves. This basic difference in approach makes all the differences between the ideas of Gandhiji and those of common men. Gandhiji's ideas and preachings struck at the root of failings of the common men. The common man finds it extremely difficult to translate his (Gandhiji's) ideas into practical life because he does not summon courage to over-power his weaknesses. Once one makes up one's mind to embibe Gandhian way of life he has to work with resolute determination. We know fully well that all obstacles melt down before a man of resolute determination. So Gandhian ideas may be difficult to translate into reality but they are not at all impossible.

It has been rightly felt that time has come to apply the Gandhian technique in Indian economy. We require a peaceful growth of our economy and the Gandhian ideas fit the bill. Our remote villages lie in pathetic conditions. We are to remove such conditions. We should create employment, avenues and abolish poverty. It is the Gandhian ideas only which can operate healthier and happier villages. Perhaps, the villages receive less attention from the elites in New Delhi and State Capitals. Once situation improves and villages are treated as desired by Gandhiji, we can wait for a golden era. So the politicians and bureaucrats must put their zeal to combat defects and shortcomings. In the villages, the cottage and small-scale industries do not get the importance they deserve. There are many such items which suit the villages alone, not the cities. We can utilise the village conditions and put the villages back to the road of rapid development. Though we lack capital, but there is no dearth of labour. We can utilise this vast untrapped sources. The example of China is there, which serves a lesson to us. We have to adopt capital-light industries with quick fruition effect. There is much less handicap in adopting labour-intensive technology rather than capital-intensive one. Keeping in view that teeming millions that we have in our country, Mahatma Gandhi had stressed upon the importance of Khadi, village and small-scale industries. His suggestion is a reply to our dual problem of paucity of capital on the one hand and abundance of labour on the other. Even today we have not been able to solve these problems to any appreciable extent. We are still short of capital and have rampant unemployment of men and material resources. In every five year plan we have been carrying the backlog of unemployed persons. For the first time in the Seventh Plan we are expecting to do a little better on this front. But if wishes were horses beggars might ride. So time alone will prove whether we are able to badge an inch more by the time Seventh Five Year Plan is over (at the time of writing). By and large we can expect the mass-scale unemployment to continue even by the close of Seventh Five Year Plan. So solution lies in having faith in the Mahatma's principles. Let us translate his suggestions into reality and have mushroom growth of Khadi, village and small-scale industries which are capital-light and labour-intensive. His suggestions, it is wrong to say, have outlived their utility. They hold good even today. Rather we should depend on them more today than we depended on them yesterday.

REFERENCES

1. Larry Collins & Dominique Lapierre, *Freedom at Midnight,* Vikas Publishing House Pvt. Ltd., Eleventh Edition 1982, p. 129.
2. Bhabotosh Dutta, *Indian Economic. Thought,* Tata McGraw Hills, New Delhi, p. 151.
3. Larry Collins & Dominique Lapierre, *Freedom at Midnight.* Vikas Publishing House Pvt. Ltd., Eleventh Edition 1982, p. 92.
4. R.R. Diwakar, *Satyagraha,* Hind Kitab Publisher, Bombay, First Edition, 1945.

2

Gandhi's Political Philosophy

Gandhiji's political philosophy is very vast, deep and concrete and, at the same time, contrary to the modern methods adopted by the politicians and so-called statesmen of today.

He was a socialist in nature. He wanted the Government to look after the people's need first. So his socialism may seem a bit radical too. He was eager to remove evils from the life of the people and the country. He did not like half-hearted attempts or some minor reforms by way of eye-wash. Specially, he wanted to root out the evils of caste-system, untouchability and exploitation of the poor.

Gandhiji's political philosophy may put people in dilemma, if his essence of thought is not properly grasped. It may lead one to take him as 'muddleheaded fool'. Because, if we call him a socialist (he himself preferred to call him a socialist), others may call him a communist too. However, if we want to call him a communist care should be taken to eliminate some elements like dictatorship of the proletariate, class-conflict and use of violent means to set up classless society, attacking the neighbour (i.e. neighbouring country), abolition of money etc. His principle was one of peace and non-violence.

Again, he may be called an anarchist too ! He did not favour too much State intervention. But he had the remarkable difference with the anarchist in the sense that he never favoured disobedience of the laws of the land and other rigorous methods over his peaceful method endowed with truth and non-violence. He clearly observed in the *Sarvodaya*, "The State represents violence in a concentrated and organised form. The individual has a soul, but as the State is a soulless machine, it can never be weaned from violence to which it owes its very existence."[1]

Critics often try to point out inconsistencies in his statements. But the fact remains that Gandhiji never changed his basic principles. However, like a perfectionist, he kept on changing and improving many of his sayings with time. Because, he was no less practical either. Horace Alexander remarked :

> "I believe that in every human being who is not seriously limited in his personality, there is in fact some element of most, if not of all, of these seemingly contradictory attitudes to life. In my own experience, at least, I have noted again and again that men who are extremely radical in their politics may be ultra-conservative in art or in some aspect of their personal lives... Now, the great merit of Gandhi is that he is such a complete man that he can recognise the need for some element of everyone of these principles in the life of the community. Without being wholly, he can and does strike a balance among them all. "[2]

The crux of the problem is that it has almost become the practice of the day to seek refuse in his (Gandhiji's) ideologies for narrow fulfilment of personal goal,—or at the most at the party level. Probably, the reasons behind such practice are that Gandhiji not only appeared very simple in his outlook but his words too were so simple that even a child could understand what he meant by saying this or that. Yet everything is so deep that it is hell of a problem for the policy-makers to adhere to what he said, be it at personal level or at party level. Sri Girilal Jain, in his article, 'The Permanent Revolutionary' has said :

> "On a superficial view, there is a folksy quality about much of what Gandhiji wrote. In fact, the simplicity is deceptive. Clearly a great deal of hard thinking went into whatever the great man wrote and spoke. Those who had the good

> fortune to listen to him will recall that he spoke with great deliberation—almost at dictation speed—as if every word mattered. And, of course, to him every word did matter. As an intensely religious man, he respected words. Have not our *rishis* said : "First, there was God and Word was with Him. Word is God." That is why he was so devastatingly effective, though he was not an orator. No wonder, he shook India as no one had done before centuries or has done ever since."[3]

To achieve a goal, a man should be morally purified. If a man, or a race or a nation has moral strength to fight for a cause for the betterment of life and growth, he or it is bound to be successful—today or tomorrow. That is why he stressed so much the purity of heart and soul combined with moral strength. In the words of Girilal Jain again— "... the moral impulse Gandhiji brought into India's political life is not dead. The Indian ruling elite may indulge in self-aggrandizement but the Indian people continue to ask for rulers who are guided by moral considerations. Indeed, the crisis of legitimacy cannot be resolved so long as morality is not accorded its proper place in the country's public life.[4]"

He was, well aware of the fact that without moral strength India cannot achieve anything viable. His very measuring rod of valuation was morality, and hence, he applied the ethics of morality in every sphere—be it economics or religion or politics. "That economics is untrue which ignores or disregards moral values. The extension of the law of non-violence in the domain of economics means nothing less that the introduction of moral values as a factor to be considered in regulating international commerce.[5]"

Gandhiji was aware of the political values of life and the nation. But he did not digest the idea of giving it undue importance. His steps and activities in the context of the freedom struggle were unmistakably political one. "My work of social reform", he said :

> "...was in no wayor subordinate to political work. The fact is, that when I saw that to a certain extent my social work would be impossible without the help of political work, I took to the latter and only to the extent that it helped the former.[6]"

However the most powerful tools in the hands of Gandhiji were his twin weapons, viz., 'Truth' and 'Non-violence' (*Ahimsa*). Gandhiji made no mistake to apply his principles time and again against the mighty 'English Power'. Perhaps this shook the English like anything and they had to quit. His truth was God and God was truth. It was not a day's outcome that Gandhiji managed to apply. Manubahen Gandhi a constant companion to Mahatma Gandhi observed :

> "We are all familiar with the rigorous experiments with truth which Bapuji had carried on for over fifty years.[7]"

But it would be utter folly on our part to consider his policy of non-violence as a policy of the meek and weak. Maybe, one has to remain meek throughout, but never weak at any cost.

Gandhiji, it is said, and in his words too, has several times expressed that he derived a lot from the Holy book, *The Gita*. In his book, *Hindu Dharma,* he says :

> "But to say that the Gita teaches violence or justifies war, because advice to kill was given on a particular occasion, is wrong as to say that *himsa* is the law of life, because a certain amount of it is inevitable in daily life. To one who reads the spirit of the Gita, it teaches the secret of non-violence, the secret of realizing the self through the physical body.[8]"

His non-violence had the purpose of changing the wrong-doers and help them put on the track of truth and righteousness. His love for the wrongdoers too was so sincere that he called his 'truth-force' as 'love-force' or 'soul-force'. That is why he laid down some conditions for the *Satyagrahis.* These conditions are, a *Satyagrahi* is not supposed to nurse hatred in his heart against those he is doing *Satyagraha.* The point at issue should invariably be true and substantial and he (the *Satyagrahi*) should be prepared to shoulder any sort of suffering for the cause undertaken, and of course till the end.

Gandhiji's simple nature is reflected in his words and deeds both. He has suggested some effective remedial measures to uphold truth and non-violence. These measures are :

(i) Civil Disobedience,
(ii) Boycott — Social, Economic and Political,
(iii) Picketing, and
(iv) Fasts.

Civil Disobedience

In *Young India,* September 13, 1919, Gandhiji mentioned in no uncertain terms about the people's action against a law contrary to the human welfare. He said :

> "I have found that it is our first duty to render voluntary obedience to law, but whilst doing that duty I have also seen that when law fosters untruth it becomes a duty to disobey it. How may this be done? We can do so by never swerving from truth and suffering the consequences of our disobedience. That is civil disobedience.[9]"

Gandhiji was undoubtedly a master in the art of practising civil disobedience. Earlier, he had proved his mettle while struggling for the rights of the blacks in South Africa. Though his actions were political in nature, the same can be applied precisely in social and economic issues as well. Here it is worthwhile to mention that it requires unflinching faith in discipline, unity and courage to suffer on the part of those who apply it. Such faith and patience are necessary because once it (i.e. Civil Disobedience) is launched, one has to face physical assaults (in the form of Lathi Charges etc.) and even shooting. But, it is at the same time very much assured that the opponent cannot stand this moral force and he gives in.

Civil disobedience is clearly a hard job, since it involves too much patience and mental struggle. Moreover, it may amount to direct struggle against the Government machinery and naturally Government machinery may resort to unfair and unlawful measures. But, it is proved that ultimately the evil power cracks.

Boycott or Non-cooperation

Boycott or non-cooperation is also a powerful tool to reach a target. During the independence struggle, people did not cooperate with the authorities and stopped purchasing of foreign articles or anything imported. This stood in good stead and brought a national consensus. Gandhiji induced the people to use home-spun Khadi and home-made salt. The world at large had witnessed the success of power of non-cooperation and boycott. Sometimes even consumers can fight injustice against unwarranted price-rise of commodities. So apart from the social, political and economic laws, people can fight injustice originating from the actions of individuals and any other groups with vested interests.

Here too, it is to be followed that boycott and non-cooperation require sacrifice on the part of individuals. Because it involves sacrifice and suffering. One may have to go without food and remuneration for days. But there is no doubt, one who persists towards the goal,—wins. Untouchability is a serious social evil. Gandhiji had to fight against this from the beginning to the end of his life. Perhaps he wanted to root out the social menace for good. Because untouchables too are human beings and deserve our full co-operation and sympathy. They are undoubtedly part and parcel of the society. We cannot ignore them. If they (the untouchables) refuse to clean cities and do other such works, it is sure to bring unbearable or serious social break-down. They too can paralyse the vehicle of life by the application of 'Boycott' and 'Non-cooperation'.

Picketing

Picketing is also a useful method to bring success in the civil-disobedience movement. Picketing can bring instant success. But non-violence should be observed in letter and spirit. Maybe, authorities concerned can apply force to break the picketing or may apply any type of measures to disperse crowd. But one should not loose patience and show resentment. So, like the other methods, here also it is necessary to be ready for suffering and other discomfort.

Fasts

Fasting is not a new concept in India. We are accustomed to it from the age of our ancestors. But Gandhiji gave it grace by using it as a means to achieve two necessary ends. "It helps in making the non-violent resister feel that he is morally better than his opponent. Secondly, the sight of a hungry man, who has refused the meals, not because he cannot get them, but in order to correct the wrong doers, wins the sympathy of the onlookers … Onlookers start imitating him slowly but surely start helping him. This brings more courage and force to the non-violent resister and finally, brings about the desired success.[10]"

Now it is obvious, fasting too is not an ordinary method to achieve success. It has got a most purifying effect on mind and body and on self and others. However it should not be used for unnecessary purposes to the fulfilment of selfish goal. Now-a-days many use it and try to purchase cheap popularity. Gandhiji certainly meant not what people are doing these days. Anyway, this is an important method of pressure on the Government or any other so-called body using unfair tactics on the people.

To be frank enough, he was very practical to discard an issue, if not suitable. He was never rigid in any sense. But his basic principles always remained intact. That is why he could say, "Non-violence in its dynamic condition means conscious suffering. It does not mean meek submission to the will of the evil-doer, but it means the pitting of one's whole soul against the will of the tyrant. Working under this law of our being, it is possible for a single individual to defy the whole might of an unjust empire to save his honour, his religion, his soul and lay the foundation for that empire's fall or its regeneration.[11]"

With the same spirit of non-violence and truth, Gandhiji blended the idea of *Satyagraha,* a unique philosophy, which, if launched for the noble purpose and with high morality, can do miracle. Before his entering into Indian Political scene, Gandhiji had proved his philosophy before the racist Pretoria regime of South Africa. It is the work of historians to study and compile those events, but to us, it clearly showed that Gandhiji never submitted before any power or to any amount of torture—physical or mental.

His *Satyagraha* was not simply an abstract doctrine, it was fully an action-oriented philosophy. It is a measure of self-suffering and holding on to truth. So truth is the basic ingredient of *Satyagraha*. One cannot deviate from the truth in any shape and must live up to that to the end. That is to say that there should be complete harmony—complete harmony in thought, word and deed. He always had observed his five cardinal vows of Truth, Non-violence, Non-possession, Non-stealing and *Brahmacharya*. The noted Gandhian, Pyarelal says :

> "Courageous, innocent suffering, by purging the emotions of the opponent of anger, fear and pride makes him more receptive to new attitudes and values. Self-purification that accrues to the *Satyagrahi* by his loving self-suffering, on the other hand, enables him to have a more understanding and sympathetic appreciation of the opponent's viewpoint; his weaknesses and redeeming virtues.[12]" It ultimately leads to

integration, identification and involvement for a nobler cause and thereby accepting suffering for truth and justice.

But here too, it should be cautioned that his *Satyagraha* too was not a child's game to be practised. One can get the idea from the version of Sri R.R. Diwakar in his book, '*Satyagraha*', where he, in very clear term, says :

> "Satyagraha is a way of life and has a system of philosophy behind it. A Satyagrahi has to follow a strict code of conduct based on self-control and loving service. Truth and Love are his guiding principles. Purification of his physical, intellectual, moral and spiritual energies, their conservation by self-control, concentration on all that is truthful and therefore beautiful and the use of his energies through active service for the promotion of peace and happiness to all, constitute in brief, the *Sadhana* of a *Satyagrahi. Satyagrahi* is always trained and ready for any emergency."[13]

Satyagraha and Passive Resistance

There is a bit difference in the meaning of *Satyagraha* and passive resistance. Many confuse them to be the same. No doubt, Gandhiji himself coined the term 'Passive Resistance', but he replaced it with '*Satyagraha*'. The reason is, passive resistance demands anger against the wrong-doer and *Satyagraha* is an action implemented through love and non-violence. There is no scope of hatred, anger, deception and untruth. Gandhiji never expressed any hatred against the English. To him, an Englishman was no less than an Indian. He was never against them as human being, he was against their practices. Many a great Indian leaders misunderstood Gandhiji on this account. He had such a child-like pure heart that—he could not dream of nursing any ill-will against any human being and even a creature. His weapon of *Satyagraha* did not mean to bring injury upon the opponent, but to convert him into an ally. Here, the passive resistance becomes a weapon of the weak and chances are there that a passive resister may resort to 'force'. So, the difference is crystal clear. One uses non-violence, truth and love and another hatred and force. *Satyagraha* is not for the weak but for the brave. Passive resistance is an instrument to be used by the weak. That is what the difference between the two and one should choose the path accordingly.

Gandhiji was a strict disciplinarian also. He never allowed loose discipline in the name of *Satyagraha* or non-violence or even in the name of Social Boycott. In the same book, *Hindu Dharma*, he says :

> "Social boycott is applicable and effective when it is not felt as a punishment and accepted by the object of boycott as a measure of discipline.[14]"

Several times it has been seen that Gandhiji received much pain when it was brought to his notice that the mass or even an individual acted with indiscipline. He himself, in spite of his simple and most ordinary life, practised exemplary discipline. That is why, he could say with least hesitation, "Complete non-violence is complete absence of ill-will against all that lives. ...Non-violence is therefore in its active form goodwill towards all life. It is pure love. ...Restraint is the law of our being. For highest perfection is unattainable without highest restraint. Suffering is thus the badge of human life."[15]

So we see that Mahatma's core of philosophy, either political or economic, was his policy of non-violence and truth; which, he adored and sometimes perfected and honed to the greatest possible extent it was possible. Because, his very philosophy was the good — 'the betterment of all'. No scientist, philosopher, economist or statesman thought in his line, he proved his each and every word to the last drop of blood. Even when he received bullets on the unfateful day of January 30, 1948, he uttered: "*He Ram ! He Ram* !" And from the words of Manubahen Gandhi, "And as he fell, his palms remained joined, as if pleading for forgiveness and mercy from the people."[16] So, in his deep dream of slumber on the lap of eternity—he forgave the wrong-doers ! Is not it comparable with the Christ or the Buddha or the Chaitanya or the Ramakrishna or the Anukula of the religious world? Even Lord Mountbatten had to say :

> "Mahatma Gandhi, will go down in the history on a par with Buddha and Jesus Christ."[17]

Again from the authors of *Freedom at Midnight* — "Mohandas Karamchand Gandhi was an unlikely revolutionary, the gentle prophet of the world's most extraordinary liberation movement. ... To a century fraught with violence, Gandhi, had offered an alternative, his doctrine of *Ahimsa*—non-violence. He had used it to mobilize the masses of India to drive England from the subcontinent with a moral crusade instead of an armed rebellion, prayers instead of machine-gun fire, disdainful silence instead of the fracas of terrorists' bombs."[18]

I cannot restrain to quote the most controversial character of Indian Freedom Struggle period, Mohammed Ali Jinnah, the creator of Pakistan,—"He was one of the greatest men produced by the Hindu Community."[19]

To conclude, I would like to add that in spite of the debate and controversial arguments to be faced, Gandhiji was definitely a most practical leader, a '*messiah*' of the suffering masses—and his politics and philosophy had only one goal—that is '*Karma*'—action,—'service to the mankind'. Last but not the least, he was very consistent in his outlook as well as in his theories. His philosophy, politics and economics are very consistent and interwoven.

REFERENCES

1. M.K. Gandhi, *Sarvodaya,* p. 74.
2. Horace Alexander, *Social and Political Ideas of Mahatma Gandhi,* p. 6.

3. Girilal Jain, 'The Permanent Revolutionary.' Sunday Review—*The Times of India*, Dated October 3rd, 1982, p. 1.
4. *Ibid.,* p. 1.
5. S.S. Gupta, *The Economic Philosophy of Mahatma Gandhi,* quotes Mahatma Gandhi, (from '*Young India*') p. 78.
6. *Ibid.*, p. 77.
7. Manubahen Gandhi, *The End of An Epoch*, Navajivan Publishing House, Ahmedabad, Ist Edition, 1962, pp. 4 and 5.
8. M.K. Gandhi, *Hindu Dharma*, Ist Edition, 1950, p. 155.
9. Shanti S. Gupta, *The Economic Philosophy of Mahatma Gandhi*, Concept Publishing Company, p. 244.
10. *Ibid.*, p. 216.
11. *Ibid.*, p. 185.
12. Pyarelal, *Gandhian Techniques in the Modern World*, Navajivan Publishing House. Edition November, 1969, p. 9.
13. R.R. Diwakar, *Satyagraha*, Hind Kitab Publishers, Bombay, 1st published 1946.
14. M.K. Gandhi, *Hindu Dharma,* Ist Edition 1950, p. 185.
15. *Ibid.*, p. 186.
16. Manubahen Gandhi, *The End of An Epoch*, Navajivan Publishing House, Ahmedabad, Ist Edition, 1962, p. 43.
17. Larry Collins and Dominique Lapierre, *Freedom at Midnight*, Vikas Publishing House Pvt. Ltd., New Delhi-2, Seventeenth Edition, 1977, p. 442.
18. *Ibid.*, p. 18.
19. *Ibid.*, p. 445.

3

Three Cardinal Concepts of Mahatma Gandhi

Varna Dharma, Trusteeship and Decentralization

VARNA DHARMA

In the Gandhian concepts, Varna Dharma occupies an important position. Varna Dharma is such a scientific social device which like that of division of labour makes the society strong, accurate and well co-ordinated. The science of *Varnashramadharma* is based on subtle scientific division of one's own profession linked with the hereditary factors. Gandhiji remarked in *Young India* :

> "*Varna* means predetermination of the choice of man's profession. The law of *Varna* is that a man shall follow the profession of his ancestors for earning his livelihood. Every child naturally follows the colour of his father, or chooses his father's profession. *Varna,* therefore, is in a way the law of heredity. *Varna* is not a thing that is superimposed on Hindus, but men who are trustees for their welfare discovered the law for them. It is not a human invention but an immutable law of nature—the statement of a tendency that is ever present and at work like Newton's law of gravitation. Just as the law of gravitation existed even before it was discovered so did the law of *Varna*."[1]

No doubt, varna is determined by birth, but it has little to do with that. A man be born a Brahmin, but may not be called a Brahmin if he does not possess the qualities of a Brahmin. "He will have fallen from Brahmanhood. On the other hand one who is born a brahman but reveals in his conduct the attributes of a brahman, he will be regarded as a brahman."[2]

But many bitter experiences have surfaced from the time immemorial to the present day. The caste-system, untouchability etc. have almost killed the beauty of the society. It pained the Mahatma like anything. He did not believe in the so-called caste-system. To him, not only truth was God or God was truth, but man in flesh and blood was an embodiment of God to him. His *Karma* (service) was always for the downtrodden and suffering masses. He was never lodged in the petty considerations of high and low castes. It was spiritual and moral progress which mattered most. In the domain of spiritual and moral progress there is no room for superiority or inferiority as such. The caste which has become the greatest obstacle for moral and material progress both, Gandhiji could not welcome it. He considered all varnas to be equal. Gandhiji could perceive things ahead of time, so he could say :

> "Varna thus conceived is no man-made institution but the law of life universally governing the human family. Fulfilment of the law would make life viable, would spread peace and content, end all clashes and conflicts, put an end to starvation and pauperization, solve the problem of population and even end disease and suffering."[3]

Divisions of Varna

Varna is divided into four groups, viz., *Brahmana, Kshatriya, Vaishya* and *Shudra*. These were meant for different services to the society. The Brahmana had the sacred duty of teaching; the Kshatriya had the valorous duty of protecting the men and material of the society from outside attack and internal disturbance; the Vaishya were the creator of wealth in the shape of business and such other relevant activities and the Shudras were supposed to offer their manual service. So it is like that of a human body which functions as a unit. If we try to dissect one from another, the human body will stop functioning. Similarly, the society as a unit may not function if the individual units do not stick to their respective duties. That is why, a proper balance, a harmonious balance has always been advocated and practised. Here again, confusion may arise to determine the respective places occupied by each division, which is sheer illusory. And, this very notion is the cause of trouble and which brings injustice and maladjustment. The very thinking of high and low is to be eradicated from the root. Gandhiji never considered the importance of one over another. To him, all were equal—as to a father or mother all the sons are of same importance. However, he had accepted the superiority of services rendered by Brahmanas, but not of their superior status. As our head is the culmination of the body, so are the Brahmanas in the four varnas. But in practical life, people tend to forget this truth and suffer from complexes. Such problems will remain so long human beings do not forget their status. Specially in the Hindus, the infighting has led to many serious problems. Many untouchables and Shudras have embraced either Christianity or Muslim religion. Gandhiji was deadly against to such conversion. The Mahatma knew it well that conversion cannot give peace but gives birth to hatred and conflict. Many incidents have so far been witnessed in Tamil Nadu, Kerala, Bihar, West Bengal and in other parts of the country also. Many died from burning, killing and underwent injuries from such conflicts. As a result of it, such people or communities accept other religions. Had we been intelligent enough to follow the Mahatma's instructions, such sad incidents were not to be witnessed. Only those people may be held responsible who suffer from their superiority complex of status.

The *Bhagvadgita* had immensely influenced Gandhiji's thinking on Varnashrama. In the Bhagvadgita Lord Krishna has said that Varnas are created by him—(चातुर्वर्ण्यं मया सृष्टम्). But

Lord Krishna's division was based on *Guna* (Quality) and *Karma* (Service or activity). Though these (the *Guna* and *Karma* factions) are to be inherited from birth alone, are definitely susceptible to one's performance—Gandhiji himself believed this and had stressed upon this several times. His views are indeed scientific and logical. We can safely place our faith in it.

Varnashrama and Interdining and Intermarriage

Throughout his life the Mahatma kept on trying to bring balance in different communities and isms. He respected the faith of Muslims and therefore, he could try for Hindu-Muslim unity. These two religions have centuries old relationship, yet they have not ceased fighting even today. But in Hindu, many socio-economic problems made a case to observe and seek Gandhiji's views. People may dine with another or may go for inter-marriage. Here Gandhiji's view is very open and clear. He admitted as follows :

> "I do not believe, that inter-dining or even inter-marriage necessarily deprives a man of his status that his birth has given him."[4]

At the same time he agreed that prohibition against inter-marriage and inter-dining was essential for the evolution of our soul. In Hinduism, one may not dine with his son or may even remain unmarried to seek salvation. So, it is up to the person concerned to act wisely or not. A Brahmana is not to lose his importance if he dines with a Shudra. What matters is that he should not exhibit his superior status before the people. So one may go for inter-marriage or may dine with anybody, provided these are not based upon superiority complex. For the purpose of spiritual goal, one may stick to strict principles as laid down in Hinduism. The essence of Hinduism is very subtle. One may not penetrate into its depth so easily as one may think of. Since, Gandhiji sought spiritual goal also, he could see it to the bottom.

Gandhiji felt that there is no question of any superior or inferior complexities to exist in Varna Dharma. He did not believe in the inherited or acquired superiority. He totally excluded the idea of superiority at any stage. According to him all are born equal. It does not matter whether one is born in India or in England or in any circumstances. Gandhiji fought the doctrine of superiority throughout his life. In order to equate himself with all, he delighted himself in calling a farmer, a labourer, a spinner, a weaver and a scavenger. He was very much against the practices of the Brahmanas who claimed themselves superior over others. He regarded it unmanly for claiming this superiority over other fellow-beings. According to him, such persons forfeit their claims to be called men.

But Gandhiji did not commit the mistake of accepting the qualities and characteristics of men to be equal. Men are born equal but they inherit a particular form or characteristics from their progenitors. So he urges us to believe in the idealistic Varnashrama, because no nation, no individual can live and prosper without ideals. We should fight the evils, if any and try to protect and understand the good in it. He declined to attach any superior status to any Varna, but he accepted higher responsibility and duties for some as compared to others. He remarked :

> "But Varna then will invest no one with a superior status or right, it will invest one with higher responsibility and duties. Those who will impart knowledge in a spirit of service will be called Brahmanas. They will assume no superior airs but will be true servants of society. When inequality of status or rights is ended, everyone of us will be equal. I do not know, however, when we shall be able to revive true varnadharma. Its real revival would mean true democracy."[5]

The religious, social and economic aspects of *Varnashrama* are a beauty in itself. One can devote to one's religious functions leading to spiritual perfection. Such a tendency is a healthy trend to develop social peace and mutual understanding. The fair distribution of wealth and abolition of social evils may result from it, if we are true to our practices. However it should be borne in mind that inter-marriage or inter-dining are subjects to one's choice. People have regulated life by practising the norms prescribed in their religion. In this way the very practice of such social habits may regulate these things and may become rigid. There is nothing to worry about these developments, unless people do not use it as their superior status or like that. Thakur Anukul Chandra of *Satsang* has remarked :

> "A guild
> composed of people
> of similar instincts—
> educated through practice
> is a Varna."[6]

I do not see any difference between Gandhiji and other Mahatmas or social reformers of India. Gandhiji made it simple and applicable. We can safely rely on what he said on *Varnashramadharma*.

TRUSTEESHIP

Gandhiji was against the unequal distribution of wealth and income in the society. The grief and suffering of the people moved him much. Like Marx and other economists and social reformers, Gandhiji was also against the exploitation of the poor by the capitalists and big business houses. The difference was that Marx advocated class-struggle but Gandhiji opposed that as it involves violence. As is known, Gandhiji never welcomed violence for any of his goals in life. His entire idea was based on truth and non-violence. He says in *Harijan* :

> "The problem therefore is not to set class against class, but to educate labour to sense of its dignity. Monied men after all form a microscopic minority in the world. They will act on square, immediately labour realises its power and yet acts on the square. To inflame labour against monied men is to perpetuate class hatred and all the evil consequences flowing from it. The strife is a vicious circle to be avoided at any cost. It is admission of weakness, a sign of inferiority complex. The moment labour recognise its own dignity, money will find its rightful place; i.e. it will hold in trust for labour. For labour is more than money."[7]

He based life on love and non-violence,—not the class-struggle. He did not want to abolish poverty and inequality of distribution through the means of violence or class-struggle. He rather expressed his willingness in favour of the capitalists to take charge of the income of the people. In the words of Dr. S.S. Gupta :

> "The capitalist who is found exploiting the people, is made the trustee of the property and so would be expected to use the property, after deducting his maximum permissible income, for the public sake."[8]

Gandhiji believed in God. He believed that God was to be found in everything. So he could not understand why a man should exploit another man when his basic needs are already met. That is why, he could say in such clear terms :

> " ... everything belonged to God and was from God. Therefore, it was for his people as a whole, not for a particular individual. When an individual had more than his proportionate portion he became a trustee of that portion for God's people."[9]

He felt that, since God created things to be used for

day-to-day purposes, human-beings too should not go for hoarding things or creating stocks. When one stocks things, he deprives others from their day-to-day use.

But the point is that it is necessary to have a high degree of morality on the part of the people. The very essence is—a high thinking coupled with plain living. Experience says that a person with plain living stands a better chance to create a favourable environment for the purpose. Gandhiji himself led an exemplary plain life—devoid of luxury and worldly comforts. His life itself serves an example to the world.

By trusteeship, Gandhiji meant welfare. People in general should get its fruits. It is not a simple task to provide welfare to all. Honesty is to be maintained at all levels. The two most important factors are his principles of truth and non-violence, which are the criteria behind it. So it is not at all necessary to pass the ownership or control to the next heir (e.g., father to son) or next kith and kin. The successor can be nominated through legal sanction, if desired. The best is to give the same to the original owner and it should be decided by the State. However a problem crops up relating to the ownership when the private property is replaced by public property. To solve this intriguing problem Gandhiji remarked :

> "That question involved some confusion of thought. Legal ownership in the transformed condition vested in the trustee, not in the State. It was to avoid confiscation that the doctrine of trusteeship came into play retaining for the society the ability of the original owner in his own right."[10]

Gandhiji had ardent faith in his non-violent method. He could say boldly :

> "My theory of trusteeship is no makeshift, certainly no camouflage. I am confident that it will survive all other theories. It has the sanction of philosophy and religion behind it. That possessors of wealth have not acted up to

the theory does not prove its falsity; it proves the weakness of the wealthy. No other theory is compatible with non-violence."[11]

Gandhiji knew the weakness of our society well. It is the poor, the exploited class, who help the accumulation of wealth by the rich. There is no doubt that without their help and participation, the rich can never become rich. Gandhiji drags in his non-cooperation principle also, which can stop the above process if followed by the people. So his non-violence and non-cooperation principles is an infallible tactics to make the trusteeship a reality.

To bring in trusteeship, difficulties may always arise. It is not an easy task to transform the rich overnight. It seems quite difficult to accept also that the rich will shed their riches off in no time. Human nature is always greedy and the very greed for wealth and riches had led to various discoveries, inventions and even economic development. The profit motive always plays a vital role behind any economic calculations. Nobody is willing to share his profit with another. The very idea is to maximise the profit. So, where economic system is based on exploitation, trusteeship may not get any response. At the most, personal appeal can be made to the exploiting class. But Gandhiji was always optimistic and he believed in persuasive tactics also. His peace loving soul at the best could prescribe a nationalisation of property and a step towards socialism. V.B. Singh rightly observes :

> "In an exploitative system trusteeship at best may be characterised as a way of personal appeal to the members of a exploiting class. Such an appeal, however, lacks the material basis to be called a rational philosophy. This also suffers from the fallacy which treats exploitation as a personal trait, and not characteristics of a social relations. This is not to deny that in isolated cases the idea of trusteeship may appeal to individuals. But if persuasion fails

to convert the exploiting classes to accept the idea of trusteeship, the Mahatma would not hesitate to quickly dispossess them without compensation. The theory of trusteeship has three steps : persuasion—failing which, state legislation or dispossession or nationalisation."[12]

In his appeal and persuasion, Gandhiji's view seems not so convincing to the rich, though it is logical and morally sound. The very beauty of his appeal is best reflected in the following lines :

> "The rich have a superfluous store of things which they do not need, and which are therefore neglected and wasted; while millions are starved to death for want of sustenance. If each retained possession only of what he needed, no one would be in want, and all would live in contentment. As it is, the rich are discontented no less than the poor. The poor man would fain become a millionaire, and the millionaire a multi-millionaire. The rich should take the initiative in dispossession with a view to a universal diffusion of the spirit of contentment."[13]

His goal of economic activities is happiness. He believed, happiness is possible, when we minimise our wants. Late Prof. J.K. Mehta of Allahabad University had also referred to the state of wantlessness. So the cause of grief and suffering is accumulation of wealth. Gandhiji wanted to disperse this centralisation or concentration of wealth. Thus the importance of trusteeship increases manifold. This may act as an instrument to bring economic order in the society.

Thus we find that in his trusteeship the principles of non-violence, truth, non-cooperation and even *Satyagraha* are present. As he was never in favour of material progress, he stressed spiritual progress. But it should be kept in mind that Gandhiji did not discard matter altogether. He knew it well that we cannot do without matter also. But his sky-high spiritual belief was that, this body is itself a matter, itself a unique mechanism of God. So one should not hanker much after the worldly pleasures and riches. Probably, Gandhiji wanted a harmonious balance in the society and that is why he lent it so much importance. He wanted everybody to labour to earn his bread and giving no room for unearned income as such.

But in practical life it is not easy to implement what the Mahatma said. *Varnashrama* divides the society according to *Guna* and *Karma* (qualities and services). We have to accept that efficiency differs from person to person. Hence payment to them may vary according to their efficiency. Even in Soviet Russia, the difference exists. Burn in his *Managerial Revolution* observes about the Soviet Union, "the upper 11 per cent to 12 per cent of the Soviet population receives approximately 50 per cent of the national income."[14] Economist Prof. S.K. Rudra also did not agree with the trusteeship theory of Gandhiji. He found it quite impracticable and spiritual. He observed :

> " ... to except people to act according to this principle though ethically supreme, actually will not render substantial and continuous results.[15]"

Before drawing conclusion on trusteeship as a principle, we must look into its long term perspective. Apparently it is improbable to put trusteeship into practice. A trustee may betray the people. But soon people may resort to non-cooperation and boycott to stop a trustee from exploiting them. It is the mass who in fact help a rich to become richer.

It has also a remarkable advantage over the capitalistic system and Marxist method of socialisation. Because in trusteeship, an owner can take that much portion of income from the trust which is just necessary for maintaining his existence only. There is no scope of misusing wealth. And in a Gandhian system, all are equal and beyond exploitation by another. Whereas in a capitalistic system, hoarding, high-spiralling income leading to inflation, injustice to the common man, centralisation of wealth etc. rule high. It is better than Marxian socialism because nothing violent is found in Gandhian method. Individual harmony, freedom of occupation, production, consumption all are present, which are not found in Marxist method of socialisation.

Thus the idea of trusteeship can be summed up as follows :

(a) It negates the right of private ownership of wealth. However a portion can be permitted to a limited scale to the trustee by the society only to help the maintenance.

(b) In the trusteeship model, production will be carried out according to the requirement of the society. No hope of profit or personal benefit or any sort of greed will be entertained.

(c) In the system, the State can regulate the business. So there is every possibility of State regulation of ownership and the use of wealth.

(d) Once it is (the trusteeship) under the state regulation, the tendency of holding or using wealth by the individual will not arise. The interest in welfare of the society will emerge in place of self-aggrandisement.

(e) In trusteeship, the income of an individual will be fixed so as to allow him to have a decent living. But the minimum and the maximum income both should be fixed. Here utmost care is necessary to see that the difference between minimum and maximum income is reasonable and equitable. It should be at the same time vary from time to time so that the difference between the maximum and minimum is negligible and becomes non-existence.

(f) So it can be said that the trusteeship may help to drive out the defects of capitalist system away and may create a favourable environment for an egalitarian society.

In the Indian context, we can apply the method of trusteeship. A proper growth of healthy economic, social and political trend in the country can take place. But we should be cautious to see that all the pre-conditions of Gandhian methods are maintained. Then we can implement Gandhian principles into practice.

DECENTRALISATION

Decentralisation concept played a pivotal role in Gandhiji's economic and political policies. From his Swadeshi movement to non-violence, non-cooperation (boycott), Khadi and Village industries, trusteeship—all are based on the decentralisation principle. His Daridranarayan—the masses lay half-starved, half-clothed and prone to all sorts of social defects and malaise. The craze for machine and machine made goods, import of foreign goods, application of labour-saving devices, introduction of sophisticated and large-scale industry has thrown the millions and millions out of their profession. Diseases have sprung up, unemployment has multiplied and many social evils have surfaced when in the name of scientific and economic progress centralisation of capital and industry has taken place. Gandhiji could not approve of such a condition. His economic ideas are meant for all—the fruits are not meant for few,—exclusively for all.

To find a befitting answer to the evil, Gandhiji propounded the idea of *Charkha* and Khadi ideology. His *Charkha*—the 'spinning-wheel' was not an ordinary instrument. He was successful in bringing a revolution and overwhelming wave which swept the country from a village to a sky-scrapper. This was such a powerful machanism in the hands of Gandhiji that it proved million times more powerful and effective than the power of a most well-trained and disciplined battalion. He could arrest the progress of the craze for machanised industry with that tiny simple *Charkha*. He advocated the use of Charkha to all and sundry. Perhaps, he meant everybody to be engaged in a gainful employment.

Not only Charkha, all sorts of village industries were stressed upon by him. India is a land of villages. But, it is the towns, not the villages which enjoy the cream at the cost of the latter. Gandhiji was truly an economist with farsightedness which was unfathomable. He studies the basic problems of Indian economics. It is little to matter even if we call it spiritual, non-violent, orthodox or village-oriented economics. He felt the need of scattering the wealth to the masses and in a proportionate manner. He was indeed a great realist. He was not in fact against the use of machines. What he meant was the way machines are being put to use. We are gradually becoming servants to machines. In a reply to a Japanese visitor Gandhiji remarked :

> "I am not against machinery as such, but I am totally opposed to it when it masters us."[16]

His idea has nicely been elaborated in his own words when he remarks :

> "When I know that even this body is a most delicate piece of machinery? The spinning wheel itself is a machine; a little toothpick is a machine. What I object to is the craze for machinery, not machinery as such. The craze is for what they call labour saving machinery. Men go on 'saving labour' till thousands are without work and thrown on the open streets to die of starvation. I want to save time and labour not for a fraction of mankind, but for all. I want the concentration of wealth, not in the hands of a few, but in the hands of all. Today machinery merely helps a few to ride on the backs of millions. The impetus behind it all is not philanthropy to save labour, but greed. It is against this constitution of things that I am fighting with all my might.[17]"

However, Gandhiji's system was opposed to the centralised political and economic power of the West. He knew the drawbacks of such system. So, he did not find a favour with them. So his views on decentralisation has received criticisms from the advocates of centralised planning. In the words of V.B. Singh :

"These two main ideas emerge :

(a) The Gandhian pattern of decentralisation is a counterpoise to the evils of centralised economy, and

(b) If machines become the servants of man, Vinoba and his associates will not object to their use. It is a pity that the Gandhians do not have adequate knowledge of :

  (i) the socialist pattern of planned society which is based on democratic centralism. Its essence is a harmonious combination of centralised direction with decentralised administration on the basis of two-way flow of communication between the 'top' and the 'bottom'; and

  (ii) the use of machine under such a system makes man the master and not the slave."[18]

But the prevailing conditions in India are not similar to those of other advanced countries of the West. The pressure of population is also an important factor to be considered. The population problem is still the greatest nuisance before the economists and planners. Because, it gives births to uncontrollable unemployment crisis. In such a juncture, it is the Gandhian model of economic policy which can come to our rescue.

Examples of few village-industries can be given which may help the millions unemployed to get jobs. Moreover, in the decentralisation policy we can adopt these simple items to be produced by the villagers at minimum cost. The capital output ratio is also negligible. These are :

Khadi

Khadi can be a great moral-booster to the millions of poverty-stricken people. The mechanism is so simple, it does not require any explanation. The cost of production and the cost of installation are meagre. So, anybody with minimum income or help from any source can establish it. The financial institutions can play an important role by providing finance. Thus the Khadi movement can be taken to every home—everybody. The Government can popularise its development and to a great extent succeed in '*Garibi-Hatao*'.

Tanning

Tanning is another occupation which can enrich our economy to a great extent. We need not export raw hide and import the finished goods made thereof. It is virtually a drain of our resources. We can enrich our technical, chemical and other branches of knowledges also. So tanning can play an important role in our economy.

Gur and Khandsari

Gur industry is a valuable cottage industry. Though sugar industry in multiplying, gur can also retain its place. Sugar is said to be a sweet poison whereas *gur* is not. Why not we should popularise the idea of *Gur* and *Khandsari* industries?

Dairy

We can supply pure and cheap milk to all through a '*goshala*'. It can be opened in the city or the villages. It can absorb some hands and supply nutritious food to the society.

Apart from the above mentioned items, many more can be taken up, viz., hand-made paper, bee-keeping, poultry etc. These involve minimum capital and simple machanism. The tremendous potentialities lie dormant in it. The society can immensely benefit from them. So, in a decentralised manner, we can inject life and energy in the economy.

So, Gandhiji's three important cardinal concepts as explained and discussed above are fit enough to give the economy a shape and of course a boosting dose towards happiness and harmony. Our very goal of life is happiness. There is no denying the fact—we all are desirous of happiness. Mere riches cannot fetch us mental peace or harmony in the society or in the economy. Perhaps innumerable examples can be cited to prove this truth. Probably everyday India receives millions of people from other countries, specially from the affluent countries. These people visit our country to seek peace, solace and happiness. But, why? They have got everything in their life yet they are unhappy. Perhaps, the truth lies in Gandhian principles. His plea for spiritual attainment was not simply for the purpose of salvation or something else. He rightly meant for our happiness. And happiness lies in the ability to limit our wants to bare minimum fulfilment of necessity only. But we happen to forget this and invite pain and incurable sufferings.

Moreover, Gandhiji ever remained a most practical personality of the world. He never placed his isms above reality. If we look at his *Varnadharma*, we find that he appeared a bit rigid in the beginning. But that was solely to uphold the importance of our ancient culture and creed. He was a great worshipper of our ancient culture. Yet he did not allow any prejudice to cloud his judgment. No anti-social element was favoured. Similarly his ideas on trusteeship and decentralisation are novel and sound. We can trust them and apply them to the best of our belief.

REFERENCES

1. *Young India*, 1927.
2. *Harijan*, 26th September, 1934.
3. M.K. _Gandhi, *Varnashramadharma*, Navajivan Publishing House, Ahmedabad, Edn. 1962, Compiled by Sri R.K. Prabhu, p. 7.

4. M.K. Gandhi, *Varnashramadharma*, (quoted in *Young India*, dated 6-10-1921, p. 317).—Compiled by Sri R.K. Prabhu, Edn. 1962, p. 35.
5. M.K. Gandhi, *Varnashramadharma*, compiled by R.K. Prabhu, Navajivan Publishing House, Ahmadabad, p. 26.
6. Sri Thakur Anukul Chandra Chakraborty, *The Message*, Satsang Publishing House, Deoghar, Bihar, October, 65, Vol.-IX, p. 17.
7. *Harijan*—October, 1935, p. 285.
8. S.S. Gupta, *The Economic Philosophy of Mahatma Gandhi*, p. 95.
9. *Harijan*, Feb. 23rd, 1947, p. 39.
10. *Harijan,* Feb. 16th, 1947, p. 25.
11. G. Dhawan, *The Political Philosophy of Mahatma Gandhi*, Ahmedabad, Edition, 1957, p. 66.
12. V.B. Singh, *From Naoroji to Nehru*, Macmillan Co. of India Ltd., Edn. 1975 pp. 126-27.
13. M.K. Gandhi, *Hindu Dharma*, Navajivan Publishing House, Ahmedabad, Ist Edn. 1957, pp. 224-25.
14. S.S. Gupta, *Economic Philosophy of Mahatma Gandhi*, p. 95.
15. K.R. Khosla, *Mahatma Gandhi, Life Through Pictures*, p. 58.
16. M.K. Gandhi, *Economic and Industrial Life and Relations,* Vol. II, Compiled by V.B. Kher, Navajivan Publishing House, Edn. 1957, p. 43.
17. *Ibid.*, p. 37.
18. V.B. Singh, *Naoroji to Nehru*, *op. cit*. Edn. 1975, p. 127.

4

Gandhiji's Views Regarding Factors of Production

Labour and Capital

Gandhiji's views on production and on the factors of production are based on economic equality. His view was that payment of wages should be based on equality. If we do not follow this, we cannot maintain economic equality. For an honest day's work the payment of wages to a doctor, to a lawyer, to a teacher and to a scavenger is to be equal. However, it literally does not mean that the amount so paid is to be equal. Wage differentials has always to be there in the society in order to give incentive to work more. We can try our level best to ensure that the gap has been reduced to a minimum. We can thus reduce the gap between the rich and the poor.

But payment to the factors of production is made according to the point reached through the interaction of demand and supply. So a factor of production cannot get more than its marginal productivity. But Gandhiji held the view that still the employer has chances of exploiting the factors by paying less to them. Thus the employer can maximise profit by ignoring even the payment of bare subsistence amount.

It seems that Gandhiji emerges as a champion of a new theory. The modern economists may think in his line and evolve suitable measures. Successfully implemented, this will halt unlawful exploitation and enrich the economy. If the profit maximisation tendency does not rule, all the factors will get better deal with regard to their remuneration. In this way, the entire process may prove very helpful to give the economy a new twist. Though Gandhiji never propounded a well-knit theory, but his ideas are useful.

From classical economists to modern economists, all have discussed the distribution problem. Adam Smith, David Ricardo, J.S. Mill of the classical school and J.R. Hicks, Mrs. Joan Robinson, A.C. Pigou and Prof. N. Kaldor have expressed their views on the subject. Marx too has expressed his clear-cut views on production and distribution. But we cannot accept the Marxian pedagogy because of its involvement in class-war and violent methods. But both wanted to rout out the evil from the capitalist system of production. In capitalist system of production, wealth and income tend to concentrate in fewer hands. Gandhiji wanted equality and welfare for all.

Gandhiji's view seems to be engrossed in spiritualism. He was dead against the conflict between labour and capital and poor and rich. He believed that no force is necessary to build a favourable environment in the socio-politico-economic system. He dreamt of a '*Ramarajya*' free from unhappiness and poverty. In Gandhian concept, economic equality is, proper housing facility for all, balanced food for all and Khadi to cover body for all. It is not the possession of an equal amount of worldly goods by all. It is, "... the master-key to non-violent Independence. Working for economic equality means abolishing the eternal conflict between capital and labour. It means levelling down of the few rich in whose hands is concentrated the bulk of the nation's wealth on the one hand and levelling up of the semi-starved naked millions on the other. A non-violent system of Government is clearly an impossibility so long as the wide gulf between the rich and the hungry million persists ..."[1]

In order to create such a favourable condition violent outburst may take place also. Gandhiji whole-heartedly opposed the idea of adopting violent means. Yet he had to agree with the Marxian concept that inequality may lead to bloody revolution also. In the words of K.R. Khosla, "The contrast between the places of New Delhi and the miserable hovels of the poor, labouring classes cannot last one day in a free India in which the poor will enjoy the same power as the richest in the land. Violent and bloody revolution is a certainty one day unless there is voluntary abdication of riches and the power that the riches give and sharing them for the common good."[2]

We can draw a line of relationship between equality and *Varnadharma*. It has been reflected in *Varnadharma* also that Gandhiji did not favour absolute equality. We are born equal means, we have the right to get equal opportunity. But, do we have equal capacity? We do not have. It is like that we cannot have height, size, weight, colour, intelligence, etc. This is never possible even in God's creation. So our ability differs from man to man. Every person is not equally gifted or talented. What one can earn by sheer brain-work, another can earn by hard physical labour. It is the talented and resourceful people who should act as trustees. A trustee can thus bring harmony by sharing his greater earnings in the society.

His views on labour and capital are not similar to Marx and other capitalist ideas. His non-violent peaceful attitude to any problem was helpful to reach the core of things. His labour was free from the shackles of capital. His disciples too were in favour of labour than to capital. His greatest follower Vinoba Bhave also had stressed much upon labour. One reason being the excessive exploitation of labour made them quite sympathetic towards labour. Gandhiji himself wanted to avoid capitalists and their multicrore activities through large-scale industry. According to Gandhiji's view, machines are such a type of process through which we too are mechanised. It is now believed in almost all quarters that the machines though create large-production but render many unemployed. It does not stop only in creating unemployment, but creates a state of idleness and intellectual deterioration. However, small-scale units are favoured in comparison since they are free from the views of large-scale industries.

There is no doubt that labour is the prime source of wealth.

The wealth of society is created by the active cooperation of labour only. Here Gandhiji had sameness of view with the classicists. And it is the labour only at whose disposal is the capital. The use of capital is only possible when it is used by the labour. So, capital is at the mercy of labour. Therefore, Gandhiji believed that labour is never under capital. He held the view that labour is the master of capital.

So labour should get its proper place in the society and in the economic mainstream of the country. It should have its role in management also. If labour is not represented in the management, then it is sheer injustice to them. As the land-tiller is the real owner of the land, so is the labour to capital. So, nobody should try to exploit labour from its very basic status. Gandhiji in *Young India* has remarked :

> "It is vital to the well-being of the industry that workmen should be regarded as equal with the share-holders and that they have, therefore, every right to possess an accurate knowledge of the transactions of the mills."[3]

In his view, one cannot accumulate more wealth than one's requirement. The idea of trusteeship is inherent here. So, labour and capital are supposed to cooperate with each other and both are not to hoard or stock than what is required. Gandhiji had the idea that the workers and peasants are supposed to remain in close liaison and must maintain an ordinary life. They must not eat or dress more than necessary. And the role of capital and labour is essentially supplementary and is to be at beck and call of each other.

To clarify the position between the owner and labour Gandhiji has thus observed in the *Young India*: "The relation between mill-agent and mill-hands ought to be one of father and children or as between blood brothers."[4] Gandhiji has thus accorded the most important place to labour for its role in production. In *Harijan* he remarked :

> "Labour possesses the key to production but lacks talent to run the mills. You could not run it even if you had a million rupees."[5]

He can be quoted again to show that labour is everything and we virtually can do nothing without labour. In the same book (*Harijan*) he remarks :

> "Capital would be helpless without labour. All mills would be at standstill, if labourers were not there to work them. There is no doubt that you are helpless without labour."[6]

Gandhiji was eager to sanction labour the rightful place in production. So, in the shape of trusteeship, labour and capital can work together to the benefit of the consumer. If the trusteeship management fails to produce any worthwhile result, the State can own or nationalise the units. But he warned also that the State-owned units should not be run for profit purpose, its goal would be to serve the human being. In such State-owned units labour can and should participate in the management. He was so liberal in attitude that he even agreed that private ownership may function provided the labour is accorded its rightful place. The labour should function as co-proprietor of the owner's wealth.

But his view has been criticised by many for anticipating such a harmony between labour and capital. They say that profit is the only aim of capitalists. But the Mahatma made very plain of it that he was : "... not a visionary. I claim to be practical idealist."[7]

Bad industrial relation is the order of the day. We know that labour-unrest and industrial-unrest are rampant these days. It is the result of the present modern state of affairs in the economy. "It is unfortunate that till recently study of the human side of labour has been criminally neglected and this had led to the present tensions, distrust and ill-will in the industrial sphere."[8]

Now-a-days labour enjoys share in profit and management,

union facilities, clubs for recreation, schools for children, medical house and residential facilities. Still many more are left to be done in this direction.

But Gandhiji's theory differs a lot from the Marxist theory. The Communists believe in class-conflict. In our tradition conflict has found no place in thinking. Gandhiji also did not allow the least possibility of conflict in the society or in between the labour and capital. The labour has always sought for a leader to guide them. But the problem is, if an ambitious, selfish and unwise leader is put, violence and strike may become a daily routine. Anyway, the condition has deteriorated in many ways. The labour and capital relationship is no more harmonious and industrial peace and price-policy too are uncertain and unpredictable. But no economy of the world has remained so far free from problems. Different socio-politico-economic systems such as Capitalism, Communism, Socialism, Nazism and Fascism have suffered from this problem. In the capitalist economy also the state is playing an important role these days. Even in the state-sector of a capitalist economy industrial relation is far from being satisfactory. In Communist countries also, there is no peace or harmony for the labour. Here labour suffers silently. Freedom of labour is a day dream in such countries. So, we see, the problem is mounting.

But Gandhiji's technique can bring peace in the society. There is no violence found in his application of different principles. He started his silent struggle from the Black Continent (in South Africa). He stood in favour of the indentured Indian labourers there in the year 1906. Again his fight for indigo peasants at Champaran is well known. In both the cases he received success and applied his principles in a larger perspective. He used the method of *Satyagraha* to bring the wrong-doers to books. It was his passive resistance in the beginning which he applied for the cause of the sufferers. Later he coined another term and replaced passive resistance to *Satyagraha*. He did not like the idea of using violent methods. For the sake of the Ahmedabad Mill workers, Gandhiji brought tremendous pressure upon the authorities. It was for the first time in India that Gandhiji organised a labour union at Ahmedabad on purely non-violent lines. So, Gandhiji was able to unite all the down-trodden from the factory workers to agricultural labourers and casual labourers.

About his labour and capital theory, Gandhiji was quite practical and up-to-date. He had a sound practical knowledge of the type of labour problems inside and outside the country. He was well-acquainted even with the western methods. So we cannot say, that his views were wrong or even unscientific. He was simply not in favour of non-violent method, rather he had realised the defects of modern machines which could hinder the satisfactory capital-labour relation. Here the method of decentralisation can also prove helpful by diversifying production in various sectors, viz. cottage industry, small-scale and large-scale industries. When the power and wealth both are decentralised, it is sure to shower the fruit of peace and tranquility in the society.

It is most heartening to note the success of Gandhiji's policies in the most advanced countries of Sweden, Japan, Switzerland etc. These countries have adopted the policy of decentralisation and have found it absolutely useful and correct method.

Gandhiji prescribed a living wage for labour which could suffice to maintain him and his family. He did not want to exceed the limit, because his very nature was against the unlimited material progress. As we all know, material progress alone cannot supply happiness. So Gandhiji was always against furthering material progress beyond a limit. Gandhi remarked :

> "I have always said that my ideal is that capital and labour should supplement and help each other. They should be a great family living in unity and harmony."[9]

Bread Labour

Gandhiji derived his idea of 'Bread Labour' from the holy book, the '*Gita*' and from the writings of Tolstoy and Ruskin. Ruskin's '*Unto this Last*' had profound influence upon the Mahatma. The Mahatma was much aggrieved to see the condition of the poor in the country. The unemployment, hunger, unrest, poverty etc. made him think for the masses. He felt that one who works (renders manual labour) has the right to eat. He believed that if the people, rich or poor, work productively for their livelihood, it becomes the 'Bread Labour'. Gandhiji foresaw in it the possibility of solving many problems connected with agriculture. In our country, the people are mostly engaged in agriculture. Hence, hardships emerging from agriculture can be easily faced if all share their labour for the purpose of production in the fields. He believed, "... invidious distinctions of rank would be abolished, when everyone without exception acknowledged the obligation of Bread Labour. It is common to all varnas."[10] The great Mahatma had realised that there was no way out from the conflict between capital and labour and the poor and rich unless we resort to such practices. He remarked :

> "There is world-wide conflict between capital and labour, and the poor envy the rich. If all worked for their bread, distinctions of rank would be obliterated; the rich would still be there, but they would deem themselves only trustees of their property and would use it mainly in the public interest."[11]

So it is necessary to earn livelihood with the help of physical labour. The physical labour thus rendered should be voluntary too. In the words of Dr. S.S. Gupta, "Thus, voluntary useful physical labour is Bread Labour. If it becomes 'intelligent' also, it becomes the highest form of social service."[12] Gandhiji mainly wanted it (the 'Bread Labour') to be linked with agriculture alone, but he did not rule out the activities such as weaving, carpentry, smithery etc. However in Gandhian concept, agriculture is to be regarded as the ideal.

The efficiency of 'Bread Labour' lies in its power of solving the unemployment problem of the country. In our country, a vast workforce remains idle. It is not the uneducated only but the educated class too can be benefited from this. "We the educated classes have lost the art of labour for one bread. With the wages of weavers, carders and spinners rising daily, there is certainly no bread problem… we must not think of earning a livelihood by desk work merely."[13] He was at the same time aware of the role of capital. As we know Gandhiji emphasised the role of labour more than that of capital and so he wanted the labour to be the master of capital and capital to be the servant of labour. He believed, "Under my system, it is labour which is the current coin, not metal. Any person who can use his labour has that coin, has wealth."[14]

The reason for Gandhiji's preference for 'Bread Labour' was that he liked the essence of physical labour. It also helps in building the moral character and promotes honest labour. It establishes the principles of truth and non-violence, plain-living and high-thinking.

Labour Strike and Trade Unionism

Labour strike is a very common feature now. In a year, millions of labour-days are lost due to *Bandh* and Strike. The trade unions often launch strike, if their demands are not met by the employers. The employers (specially the giant-owners of large-scale multi-crore units) declare closure. It is the poor labourers only who suffer maximum, sometimes it is the trade unions who apply 'work-slow' tactics and embarrass the Government or the employers seriously. This results in less production, less income, scarcity and price-rise. Though Gandhiji favoured trade-unionism, his view was that of creation of welfare of the people. He lent his support to trade-unionism to ensure that labour gets fair treatment. He meant moral and intellectual upliftment of the labour. So he advocated the labour to be the master of the means of production. But everything is to be done through the peaceful means of non-violence and non-cooperation. The trade unions, the Mahatma maintained, should not get involved in politics. He set preconditions for strike :

1. The cause of the strike must be just.
2. There should be practical unanimity among the strikers.
3. Strikers should never depend upon public subscription or other charity.
4. A strike is no remedy when there are other labourers to replace the strikers.
5. Stikers must fix an unalterable minimum demand and declare it before embarking upon their strike.
6. There is no room in a non-violent strike for violence in the shape of intimidation, incendiarism etc.[15]

So Gandhiji has suggested very useful means to stop violent practices by the workers' union. The worker unions of our time can study and apply his methods for the benefit of society.

About the labour-capital conflict, Gandhiji believed that it was nothing but greed in the part of both which causes conflict. That is when one wants to amass more than one's requirements, conflict takes place and tension is created. He made it clear that both labour and capital are useless without the other. So, in his *Harijan*, Gandhiji gave a fine warning to both by saying :

> "Labour possesses the key to production but lacks talents to run the mills. You could not run it even if you had a million rupee."[16]

And again he observed :

> "Capital would be helpless without labour. All mills would be at a standstill, if labourers were not there to work them. There is no doubt that you are helpless without labour."[17]

Thus in the age of mechanization and craze for more and

sophisticated equipments and labour saving devices, the world is heading for a grave danger. The importance of labour is being reduced now. It is obvious that the machine will drive out the labour any moment. Or the function of labour will be reduced to the minimum. Unmanned machines are showing miracles and rendering the man useless in many places. We are already in the fifth generation of computer stage where labour has got minimum to say. The giant companies are manufacturing '*robots*' to handle all the works to be done by manual power or labour. It has got its advantages also over the human labour. The advantages are as follows :

(a) Such systems can work for longer hours in comparison to human labour.
(b) No problem of labour-strike or labour-unrest is there.
(c) The cost of maintenance is also negligible when compared to the payment for human labour.
(d) It can work faster (say, with tremendous speed) and more efficiently than human labour.
(e) The production increases and cost of production is also very low.

So in the above light one can presume that the very problem or relationship of labour and capital being minimum, one need not worry. It apparently seems so. But before we agree to this, we must look into the defects too. The defects can be summarised as follows:

(a) It will create severe and chronic unemployment in the economy.
(b) Huge capital and high-grade technical know-how are the prerequisites which the poor undeveloped and developing nations cannot provide.
(c) Where the economy is burdened with over-population, such a device may create many unseen problems.

(d) A minor fault in operation may invite untold destruction of men and material.

Hence, 'all that glitters is not gold' is a correct saying. Moreover, we are supposed to solve problems of the economy, not to create them. We must adopt the suitable measures required for our own conditions. Here lies the superiority of Gandhian methods. Without disturbing the system, his was the most effective peaceful tool to bring harmony and balance in the economy. The Mahatma wanted to see the country prosper in a non-violent peaceful way with cooperation from all the ingredients of production in an economy.

In this way me see that Gandhiji was in favour of mutual harmonious relationship between labour and capital and the entrepreneur. He advised the employers to consider the labour as the real owners. His whole-hearted appeal for the cause of labourer was not unjust. In the rapidly advancing present age we see several such examples where the labourers have been accorded the ownership and rightful place in management. Gandhiji's foresightedness was amazing. What he advocated as a simple, plain-living and peace-loving soul has been increasingly adopted in practice in advanced nations of the world. Industrial democracy is becoming a reality day-by-day. He suggested that in case of a strike, labourers should be given full control of the concern. "This psychological treatment will satisfy, to a very great extent, the acquisitive nature of the labourers and relieve tensions. Scandal Plan of U.S.A., and the experiments of Yugoslavia, West Germany, France, Sweden and U.K. in the workers' participation in management have been started with this purpose in view."[18]

He was really a great 'practical idealist' who left no stones unturned to advocate harmony between labour and capital and thereby ensuring a proper balance in the economy.

REFERENCES

1. K.R. Khosla, *Mahatma Gandhi's Life Through Picture*, p. 58.
2. *Ibid.*, p. 58.
3. *Young India*,16th Feb. 1921
4. *Young India*, 10th May, 1928.
5. *Harijan*, 7th Nov., 1936.
6. *Ibid.*
7. *Young India*, 11th Aug, 1920.
8. S.S. Gupta, *The Economic Philosophy of Mahatma Gandhi*, Concept Publishing Company, New Delhi, p. 117.
9. *Young India*, 20th Aug., 1925.
10. M.K. Gandhi, *From Yervada Mandir*, Navajivan Publishing House, Edn. June, 1980, p. 24.
11. *Ibid.*
12. S.S. Gupta, *Economic Philosophy of Mahatma Gandhi*, p. 70.
13. *Young India*, 25th Aug., 1921.
14. D.G. Tendulkar, *Mahatma*, Vol. III, p. 169.
15. *Young India*, 15th Feb., 1921.
16. *Harijan*, 7th Nov., 1936.
17. *Ibid.*
18. 'Gandhian Technique and Tradition', Research Divn. All India Inst. of Social Welfare and Business Management, Calcutta. Appendix V, pp. 204-17.

5

Mahatma's Ideas on Agrarian Re-Organisation

Even today more than 70 per cent of Indians directly or indirectly earn their livelihood from agriculture. Very few people are engaged in the industrial sector. Still the number of workers engaged in the industrial sector has not increased considerably. As per 1951 statistics, 72 per cent of the people were cultivators or labourers. The number of agricultural workers has not yet receded much. In view of its importance in the national economy many fruitful measures have so far been taken in the field of agriculture. The Government has tried to bring in institutional and technological changes. Many administrative measures were taken to improve productivity and to minimise exploitative conditions. But all the measures were not introduced satisfactorily. Specially land ownership problem has remained and the poor farmers have not benefited much. The number of agricultural labourers has increased from 19.7 per cent in 1951 to 26.3 per cent in 1971. So a number of marginal farmers lost their ownership of land to the middle and rich farmers and have become agricultural labourers. About the production in agriculture it may be said that output both of food crops and commercial crops has increased. It has been possible due to increase in agricultural inputs. But the production in the field fluctuates owing to vagaries of the monsoon. However the gross production has increased from 55 million tons in 1951 to around 153 million tons in 1980. But it is felt, the yield per acre in our country is one of the lowest in the world. Many developed and even underdeveloped countries have high yield as compared to India. But this has not helped India to solve her unemployment problem and poverty. In spite of the self-sufficiency on the food front, hunger and poverty still persist. What a glaring disparity ! Obviously Gandhiji did not want this. Gandhiji held the view that 'all land belongs to Gopal'. So there should not be any starvation or problem arising from ownership. He was in favour of the actual tillers. To him actual tillers are the real owners of land. It is the tillers, the peasants who create wealth on the land. Without the active cooperation of the peasants land cannot produce anything in return. However, he suggested that land could be held in cooperation by both—the tillers and owners. This can possibly save labour, capital, tools etc. In the words of R.K. Prabhu, "Cooperative farming of his conception would change the face of the land and banish poverty and idleness from their midst. All this was only possible if people became friends of one another and as one family. When that happy event took place there would be no ugly sore in the form of a communal problem."[1]

Agriculture being the life in the economy, we are to venture for solid measures. If we can keep the food problem under control, we can strive for the betterment of the lot of the peasants. It is natural, if the people can get belly-full of square-meal daily, they can improve life in all spheres. Hunger is a curse in the society. A hungry nation can never boast of its economy. Gandhiji wanted to improve the food production by all means. He has advised a lot to improve the fertility of soil. He has advised the peasants to use very simple methods for the purpose. He did not like the use of chemical fertilizer. He was aware of the defects of chemical fertilizers. To increase soil-fertility, we can use organic manures. He suggested ways to procure manure in simple methods. He was very much fond of using simple and natural methods. Interestingly, one may quiver his nostrils when hears his plan. Everybody knows that human excreta can act as good fertilizer, yet nobody takes that plunge. But this valuable and rich manure is being wasted, inviting diseases. Prof. Brultini in 'The Use of Waste Materials' says :

"Nitrogen derived from the 282,000 residents of Delhi is sufficient to fertilize a minimum of 10,000 and a maximum of 95,000 acres".[2]

Gandhiji discussed in detail the process to make use of human waste. He suggested how much to dig the soil—its length, depth and breadth. He meant to solve many problems of the villagers by this. This will ensure better health, rich crops and material well-being. It is not necessary to go in details about the process.

In addition to human-waste, we can use cow-dung and ash also. Plenty of ash may be made available from wood (when used as fuel) and other sources. So far the question of cow-dung is concerned, everybody knows how to use. Cow-dung too is one of the best kind of manures we know. It is never advisable to use it as fuel.

Gandhiji advised the use of farm waste (or *Kuchra*) also. If we do not use them it will be a loss to the agriculture. The following can be made into compost, viz., weeds, stalks of cotton, rape, black and green gram, sugarcane trash, stools of jwar, maize and sugarcane, fallen leaves of trees, uneaten residues of grass, straw, jwar and other fodders. These are very ordinary items and always go unused and unnoticed. We can make a proper use of them and profit immensely from them.

Sometimes water too is misused or left unused due to our ignorance or lack of interest. We can dig small pits near compost area to hold house-hold waste-water. It is estimated that about 50 to 60 four-gallon tins of water can make one cartload of compost easily. It is nothing on the part of a farmer to use water in this prescribed manner. This is most simple a method which is full of promises.

Gandhiji further suggested that we can use the urine of cattle also as manure. The urine of cattle is rich in valuable manurial matter and can be used in the field as top-dressing in any irrigated crop. The process is easy and cheap. We need not make a *pucca*-floor in the cattle-shed which is costly and unsuitable.

Instead, a soft, warm and dry bed can be made with loose earth. We can use threashing-floor sweepings, silt from choked drain and earth from silage pits for the purpose. The urine will be nicely absorbed if a flat 6 inches layer is given. We can remove this layer of urine earth after four months and can use it direct in the field.

Thus it is observed that there are numerous ways of using natural fertilizers which can enrich our economy to a great extent. These methods are indeed very simple to use, yet can produce invaluable results. However, a scientific age has been ushered in and everybody is seriously inclined towards it. Large fertilizer factories are producing million tons of chemical fertilizers now. The farmers too are busy in purchasing and using them for their fields. These fertilizers give quick results and increase the magnitude of production also. Now many favour the use of these fertilizers. In order to ensure huge amount of food production, the Government is even importing fertilizers. But we can see the other side of the coin also. Chemical fertilizers gradually destroy the fertility of land. More and more use of it is rendering the lands less fertile for future. The food thus grown is losing the natural test also. So, it is always advisable to implement the examples of Mahatma Gandhi in best of spirit and deed.

If we are desirous of getting better quality food and its natural taste, we must eat the food accordingly. The growing use of chemical fertilizer has already robbed the food of its naturalness, so we must see that we eat the food which retain the food-value to the maximum possible extent. For example, if we form the habit of eating unpolished rice instead of polished rice, it will help our rice-pounding sisters as well as we shall get better food-value out of it. Similarly, we can eat whole-wheat flour instead of fine flour. The whole-wheat flour contains nutritional value more than fine flour. These simple but valuable measures will ultimately enrich our agriculture and agriculturists. The farmers and villagers and village-industries will be also benefited out of it.

The issue of mechanisation of agriculture is another problem. We can try Gandhian methods to fight the evil of mechanisation. Mechanisation has taken place everywhere now. Not only in the developed western countries, in the Asian countries also, the craze for mechanisation is rampant. But we are aware of the evils of the mechanisation in no uncertain manner. Lord Northbourne warns in his book 'Look to the Land': "mechanization can be a terrible snare, as it makes possible the kind of soil exploitation which has led to desert making on a scale hitherto unparalled."[3] So, there is no way out from the evils of mechanisation also. "In Egypt, it has been observed that fertility of soil deteriorated by the increasing use of efficient technique."[4] The remedy hence is to get rid of the process of mechanisation. In the words of Lord Northbourne again :

> "The very best in farming as in all other crafts can only be produced by hand, and less the best will not do."[5] The defects of mechanisation can be understood if we consider a case of using tractor in a piece of land. There is no doubt that a tractor can till the land more quickly than hand plough. But it results in rendering many off the field and off the job. Those who were so far healthily employed would turn jobless. They would definitely try other unhealthy jobs in factories or mills. The West too is realising the truth that mechanization does not help much. ... "agriculture in many Western countries has gradually fallen into the hands of engineers and chemists, who from the first set about their job in a forthright manner. First came the sacrifice of fertility by the wrongful disposal of vegetable and human wastes, then chemical feeding of the soil, and finally, specialized, commercial farming with pressurised food production from soil, plant and animal. The techniques of specialized farming, like those of industry, drive more and more workers into routine jobs, thereby destroying their sense of

vocation, while the heavy costs of such farming tend to drive agriculture into the control of financiers.[6]"

The seriousness lies in the very fact of creating unemployment by the machines. The hand plough though takes a long time to cover a plot of land, it is still welcome in the Indian agriculture. It is not only simple but it is less costly and can be utilized in the smallest plot of land also. The question of pollution is also there. The hand plough does not pollute the environment, but a tractor does. So after highlighting both the sides, we have to agree that Gandhian method is more reasonable and welcome. Besides, India is a huge country with the heaviest burden of population. So labour saving technique is not so welcome.

Cattle is also an indispensable part of agriculture. But the condition of cattle is very poor in India. The present world is showing more willingness for collective or cooperative farming. The poor farmers are not in the position to maintain their cattle. Their land holding are so fragmented that they do not help them to keep cattle. To find an answer to this, we are bound to look at cooperative measures.

(a) In the collective system, the farmer need not keep the cattle with him. It is unhygienic also to live together with animals. So the space so vacated can be used for other purposes.
(b) Secondly, with the increase in number, the farmer is either bound to sell or kill them. Even if he keeps them, cannot feed. So in a cooperative system the defect can be tackled.
(c) In case of disease, a poor farmer cannot arrange for veterinary treatment. But he can solve this problem if the cooperative system is there.
(d) For a better breeding one selected bull can serve the purpose for many. But a farmer as an individual may find it hard to afford.

(e) In the cooperative system, a common grazing ground may be available for the cattle. The individual farmer cannot do this.

(f) In the system of large-scale economy, expenditure on fodder will be less. This is another monetary benefit.

(g) The income from milk-sale will be helpful to the farmer. This will benefit the society also. The consumer will also get pure and cheap milk, not adulterated milk as could be the case if the individual farmer would have sold it.

(h) In collective system, efficiency of the cattle can be examined from time to time. This was not possible for the individual farmer to do.

(i) So the cooperative system is a unique system of its own. It was impossible of the farmer to do justice to him or to the cattle as well.

Thus we see that we can bring successful agrarian revolution by launching various measures. Cattle is part and parcel of agriculture. If we neglect its well-being, the entire agriculture will suffer. So it is necessary to resort to cooperative farming. We can cultivate our lands also through this method. In this method, individuals are not required to run after their plots individually. The land will be collectively cultivated and the income/produce will be divided accordingly. Individuals can easily safeguard their independence in the cooperative system.

But the condition of agriculture in India is so deplorable that we feel ashamed of our scientific and technological progress. Some of the problems can be taken up and Gandhian remedial measures applied :

(a) The foremost problem is fragmentation of land holding. So small land holdings are there that we cannot imagine how a plough and bull can move in that. The root of the problem is that from the age of ancestors lands are being divided and subdivided and the process is being continued till the present generation. It renders the land quite uneconomic in size to be cultivated. The cost of production also increases. Dependence in the same portion of land by many creates the problem of unemployment and disguised unemployment. All are seemingly engaged in cultivation, but the marginal productivity of labour over a wide range is zero. To elucidate, even if quite a few persons are removed from the field of agriculture, total productivity will not go down. This is a threat to the existence of the farmer. We have to resort to co-operative farming to make it meaningful. The rest of the members of the same family can start cottage or small-scale industries with minimum expenditure and technical knowhow. Or, as suggested by Gandhiji, there are abundance of village industries for this purpose. These industries neither require heavy finance nor any technical expertise. Moreover, there is no question of disguised unemployment or seasonal unemployment. Thus it is not difficult to solve the problem created by fragmentation of land.

(b) Uncertainty of water or inadequate water supply is another problem. In India, monsoon is said to be most uncertain. It may or may not rain. It may rain too much causing flood and famine or it may rain too less causing drought and famine. To combat this problem, we try the resources available with us. If river or pond is there, we can try to use the water by cutting canal or joining the fields with drain. If well-knit irrigation facilities can be arranged like that of the Punjab, any climate condition can be boldly faced. Where none are possible, we may take the help of wells and tube-wells. In all the cases, we have to arrange alternative measures to fight the problem. If it leads to less production, Gandhiji advised us to resort to less eating and understanding between vegetarians and non-vegetarian. For example, a meat-eater may not eat pulses, oils and such other items to help his vegetarian fellows to fight the situation. Moreover, if required, one may eat fruits. Fruits are very good items of food and at times can substitute bread or rice even. So, this problem of water can also be successfully tackled.

(c) To get a better deal from our lands, we should take suitable measures to improve its fertility. Gandhiji has devised a number of measures through which we can improve the fertility of land. We have already studied that aspect of land. Still, we must take proper care of the land to get maximum out of it. If we take care of land, land will take care of us. We can apply different type of natural manures to increase the fertility of land. We have to stop the process of soil-erosion also. If land continues to erode, it may be a cause of grave concern indeed. We have to try for tree plantation to stop this problem.

(d) To fight any problem is not an easy task. It cannot be handled single-handed. So, the device of cooperative method is there. We have already studied the merits of cooperation and have come to the conclusion that cooperative method of farming can solve many problems. Specially in the Indian context, it may improve the total output of food grains and other crops. It may also help to produce more milk, vegetables etc. Anyway, it is able to solve a number of problems relating to agriculture.

(e) There may be cases when we may need the help of the State. Though Gandhiji disliked too much interference, but he felt it necessary in the view of poor condition of the agriculture. Sometimes, the aid and protection are very much necessary for survival of certain crops in certain time. If famine sets in, it is not possible to fight the issue quite effectively without the State-aid. Sometimes protection is also necessary.

(f) To improve the agrarian scene of the country, there should be reclamation of land also. But Government help is necessary to do the needful. Thousands of acres of salty-lands near the different coastal areas are lying unused. As stated, this is not possible for a private agency to tackle it or take up the issue.

Thus we see that we need to form cooperative societies for the various activities connected with agriculture. The villagers are required to promote group efforts to bring a peaceful and fruitful change in their life. It is the cooperative societies which help to stock and market raw materials, distribute seeds, tools, manures, etc. We have to increase the food production so that everyone gets food and everybody gets absorbed in jobs. Few more points are to be borne in mind that we have to increase the irrigation facility so that maximum area can be covered under this. About manure we are to remember it that we need not go far, rather should try to stop the wastage. In the village sweepings, bones, human excreta etc., remain unutilised. We can utilise them as a good quality of compost manure. Oil cakes are often exported. Oil cakes can be used as a good fertilizer. To stop this we can use the oil-seeds in the local country *ghanis*. This may help in retaining both oil and cake enriching the village and villagers. Care must be taken for proper management of land. We should try to stop soil erosion by all means. Proper drainage and embankments are necessary for the purpose. The modern age is the age of research and development. So research work is necessary to improve food crops, high and quick yielding varieties of seeds. Selected and thus improved varieties of seeds are necessary for the increase in production.

So, these above discussed points are some fundamental drawbacks of our agriculture. It is definitely not curable by individual efforts only. Only the State can come to the rescue. So the State can deal such issues in time and effectively.

Thus we see that the State too has an important role to play in eradicating the problem of the agriculture. Individually, only minor problems can be solved, not big problems involving huge sum and technical knowhow.

Through the agrarian re-organisation we mean to bring a state of independence on the food front. Here food does not mean rice or wheat only. In the food category, from the cereals to fruits all are included. Again, it encompasses those crops also which clothe us also. We want to stop hunger and provide clothes to all. That is why a very sound agricultural policy is required to be built in the Gandhian line. Gandhiji was wise enough to understand the real situation of our agriculture and economy as a whole. His basic idea was to provide food and cloth to each and all. Once the people have sufficient to eat and clothe, there basic needs are almost fulfilled.

At the present stage of our economy, we are self-sufficient in both. But the irony is, we are not walking along the Gandhian line. It is only in the name that we follow him and advertise his novel principle. Gandhiji was so much a peaceful, a non-violent soul that he dreamt a Heaven for his people. He did not mean that there should be only sufficient food and cloth, but he meant that all should be engaged in work. There should not be unemployment and related problems arising from this. He also did not mean a polluted environment, polluted water and a serious existing threat to ecological balance. So, problems are in fact not solved as such. Problems are rather going to take serious shape. Still time is there and still we can resort to Gandhian practices to bring a harmonious growth through the agriculture.

REFERENCES

1. M.K. Gandhi, *India's Food Problem*, Compiled by R.K. Prabhu, Navajivan Publishing House, Ist Edn., April, 1960.
2. *Harijan*, 15th March, 1935, p. 36.
3. M.K. Gandhi, *Food Shortage and Agriculture*, Navajivan Publishing House, Ist Edn. 1949, p. 199.

4. *Ibid.*, p. 200.
5. *Ibid.*
6. Wilfred Wellock, *New Horizons: Build the Future Now*, Housemans' Bookshop, London N. 4, p. 81.

6

Gandhi and the Controversy of Large versus Small-Scale Industries

With Special Reference to Khadi and Gramodyog (Village Industries)

The large-scale and small-scale controversy in Gandhian thought has so far drew many economists to study the matter in details and scrutinize it closely. Many misleading explanations have also been given. However the Mahatama himself kept on changing his views, which in fact made people to believe that his concept was not clear and correct. But a close look will reveal, that neither of the complaints are correct. He in fact never drifted away from his basic concept. His basic concept was that of non-violence and truth. Throughout his life he did his best to change the plight of the poor, the general mass. His peaceful non-violent measures were aimed at the betterment of life for all. His welfare view was for all—not confined to a limited group of people. He was so generous that he could think for anything only in the terms of all—the mankind. His welfare view was not restricted to a particular time or place either. So time and again, the Mahatma has been misunderstood by us.

He was in favour of welcoming improvement at all stages of development—in man and machines alike. However he was always doubtful of great use of machine. He suspected that it would harm the society. He was not wholly against the use of machines but the growing importance of the use of machines led him to think otherwise. He went deep into the root of the problems of the use of machines and consequently its effect upon the peace and happiness of the people. He accepted its use to the extent it helps human-being to maximise peace and happiness. His non-violent principle was always after seeking the best adjustment between man and machine. But the trend of industrial progress was such that simple machines were replaced by more complicated and big machines. The very nature of industrial progress has led to the idea of higher production, massive accumulation of wealth, exploitation of labour etc. The amazing scientific progress has brought manifold worldly material pleasures at our door steps. Communication through satellite has reduced the time and distance barrier. People are almost in physical touch with the remote parts of the globe—which was hitherto possible in imagination or thought-wave only. But the capitalist world has taken stock of the situation. They are going to create anything they wish to produce for the sake of fancy. The result has been the exploitation of the poor. Exploitation is the most important cause of suffering of the poor. Gandhi in *Young India* remarked :

> "What is the cause of the present chaos? It is exploitation, I will not say, of the weaker nations by the stronger, but of sister-nations by sister-nations. And my fundamental objection to machinery rests on the fact that it is machinery that has enabled these nations to exploit others."[1]

Gandhiji was opposed to such exploitations. He treated exploitation as inhuman and violent. He felt that the mass cannot derive peace from this. If the capitalist process is continued unhindered, it may make the rich richer and the poor poorer. Excessive industrialization is also bad. The country concerned should be able to neutralise the bad effects emerging from it. The present impact of the industrial sector on our economy is like this :

"India's high cost industrial sector has harmed the country in more ways than one. It has added to inflationary forces, impeded exports, reduced the rewards of high savings and investment ratio and slowed down economic growth."[2]

It seems that he was against the use of machinery. But it was really not so. He clarified the matter in a reply to a question of a disciple of Rabindra Nath Tagore whether he opposed all machinery. His reply was, "How could that be possible? I know that my own body is nothing but an extraordinarily delicately constructed machine. The spinning wheel is also a machine, ... I am not fighting against machinery as such, but the madness of thinking that machinery saves labour."[3]

So it is very much explained that his objection is to what machinery does. It saves labour. If labour is not required, labour is unemployed then ! So the labour-saving utility of machines was not important for him. To be frank, he did not oppose the idea of using machines. He was a saint like man, who wanted his country men to be happy and prosperous. If the people remained unemployed, the idea of happiness does not hold good. If machines come in the way, Gandhiji was ready to abandon such machines. Such machines had no use for him.

In fact, there was no controversy between the large-scale and small-scale industries in the Gandhian concept. From his very explanation it can be safely inferred that Gandhiji was neither against the large-scale nor against the small-scale industries. His point of view was that, be it large-scale or small-scale, it should not rob the labour of its due. There should be peace and harmony in the society. We can link his concept with large-scale, small-scale and cottage industry. If the trio complement each other and help to establish peace and harmony in the society, it is indeed very useful. Many a time question had been put to Gandhiji whether he approved of the functioning of large-scale industries. Gandhiji was of the view that if such industries are essential for the existence of the country and people, we are to accept them. When Gandhiji accepted the usefulness of Singer

Sewing Machines, he was asked to give his opinion about the establishment of factories to produce Singer Sewing Machines. He expressed his view in affirmative. But his condition was that such machines should be under the State (nationalised). Thus he silenced his critics who took him to be against such industries.

Since the problem of unemployment is acute in the country, (that time it was not so, yet he) he wanted everybody to be engaged in gainful employment. That is why, the labour-saving machines were not liked by him. In the villages, where people are more backward and remain unemployed throughout the year, he stressed the need for development in small and cottage industries. His village industries were able to remove the backlog of unemployment. His ideas behind Swadeshi movement, establishment of *Charkha* at every household, was meant to make the people self-reliant and economically sound.

He was really very unhappy over the glaring poverty of the people. So he remarked in *Young India* :

> "At the lowest estimate 80 per cent of the population of India is agricultural. This makes over 24 crores. It is well known that during half the year this population remains practically idle or has at least many hours at its disposal for useful work. If this population is given an easy, substantial and profitable word to do, one of the highest economic problems will have been solved. In my humble opinion, such an occupation is hand-spinning. It can be easily learned by everybody and it is most perfect way in my opinion of utilising the idle hours of the nation."[4]

Charkha is a unique instrument. This can be established at every home and employment can be created to a great extent. This is such a simple spinning machine that it can be handled by anybody—even a layman. *Charkha* served a double purpose for Gandhiji. It was politically a most powerful means to unite the whole country and in the point of view of economics, *charkha* and khadi was a sort of revolution in the line of small-scale industries.

His *Charkha* and Khadi were a concept, powerful enough to solve the problem of future also. The mounting population problem has created such a havoc that land-holding in the villages and jobs in industrial sector are diminishing. It can provide livelihood to millions. The diseases of disguised and seasonal unemployment can be cured by this simple spinning wheel. It was not an instrument of the weak. It was neither an old system. It was completely a Gandhian way of solving problem. His *Charkha* was misunderstood and criticized by many big shots of the time also. Even Gurudev Rabindra Nath Tagore expressed his severe doubt about its capacity to solve the problem. But the Mahatma was unmoved. He continued his journey of non-violent peaceful struggle till the end of the mortal frame. He observed in *Young India* :

> "Khadi was once the dress of the nation at large ... There are instances of whole villages taking a legitimate pride in the fact they had to import nothing but salt in the whole round of six seasons. With such conditions, there could be no drain, no exploitation and therefore, no para-*raj* (others rule)."[5]

If the people can struggle in non-violent way, they can do miracles. The weapon of truth and non-violence has immense power. It can shake the foundation of the mightiest empire of the world. It requires that courage—the boldness of truth to fight. His Khadi was not an ordinary dress. It was the symbol of national integration and harmony.

Gandhiji wanted that we should produce our own clothes. We required nearly 13 years of cloth per head per year, but we failed to produce that much even. It is indeed a pity for the people of this country. But hand-spinning can solve this problem. It can provide clothes to millions. It is shocking that though India produces sufficient cotton but millions of bales of cotton are exported and we get manufactured clothes back from those countries. Since India is capable of producing her entire requirements through hand-weaving and hand-spinning, this unique cotton industry (hand-spinning) can give employment to millions. So the Swadeshi principle can go a long way to solve India's poverty.

He was against the colonial exploitation and he therefore advocated the Swadeshi movement. It was not an ordinary movement or a narrow nationalism. This was based on his ideology of non-violence and removing the colonial exploitation. His ideology of *Swadeshi* served the double purpose of political freedom and economic development. It was strictly aimed at removing the foreign goods and encouraging the indigenous products. He took the unique vow of destroying the entire foreign clothes in his possession and use only clothes made from Indian cotton. He said :

> "... I shall confine myself, for my personal requirements, to the use of cloth, manufactured in India from Indian cotton, silk or wool and I shall altogether abstain from using foreign cloth and I shall destroy all foreign cloth in my possession."[6]

He was very much practical man and he observed the degradation of national products. So he knew what Swadeshi can do arrest the exploitation of our national wealth. So he warned, "It is the greatest delusion to suppose, that the duty of *Swadeshi* begins and ends with merely spinning some yarn anyhow and wearing Khadi made from it. Khadi is the first indispensable step towards the discharge of Swadeshi dharma to society. But one often meets men, who wear Khadi, while in all other things they indulge their taste for foreign manufactures. Such men cannot be said to be practising *Swadeshi*. They are simply following the fashion."[7]

He wanted the country to be strong, based on strong foundation. It was not so much to keep the country aloof from others. It was simply a very powerful device to help the country emerge more sound and self-reliant. He was very realistic to point out that our resources should not be exported to Europe and other countries. Because in this way we are losing our valuable assets. So once this *Swadeshi mantra* becomes a household affair, millions of people will find a new life. It will open the door for economic salvation. He was afraid that the blind imitation of English economics would not lead us anywhere, rather would damage our prospect seriously. He was definitely keen to uplift our living-standard also. Through the Swadeshi movement we could get both, the political freedom and economic advancement. Here he sounds similar to that of the German economist Friedrich List. In favour of Swadeshi cloth Gandhiji expressed as follows :

> "If crores of people will refuse to wear or use foreign cloth and be satisfied with the simple cloth that we can produce in our homes, it will be proof of our organising ability, energy, co-operation and self-sacrifice that will enable us to secure all we need ... It can only be achieved by new production and judicious distribution."[8]

Swadeshi dharma in essence is to utilise one's own resources. Though economists like Prof. W.A. Lewis considered the Gandhian approach as anti-growth. It does not hold good. Gandhian approach was for the peace, moral and spiritual progress of the people based on the non-violence and truth. Thus we see that in present delicate situation of the world peace, Gandhiji's principles are quite relevant in the present state also.

There are numerous items of village-industries which can turn our villages self-reliant in all aspects. It is a pity that the villages look forward to the cities for every petty item. If we follow the Gandhiji's advises sincerely, we can turn the villages not only to be self-sufficient but also to be progressive in outlook. It is the villages who supply everything to the cities and in lieu get poor payment not sufficient enough for their sustenance even. Not only this, things thus produced by the mills and factories of big cities, lack naturalness and healthy substance. For example, Khadi clothes compared to mill-made clothes, oils from *ghanis* compared to mills, etc., are more welcome to the villages. For the reason of capital also, the production of different items in the village environment suit them very much. Simple tools, simple technical know-how, meagre capital can be of immense help. So we should try to improve the condition in the villages in the following ways :

(a) Cotton, sugarcane, soyabean and grain are to be produced under improved methods.
(b) The use of Dhenki and Chakki to be revived for husking paddy, grinding wheat and breaking pulses.
(c) Ghanis and Kolhus to be revived for producing oil and gur respectively.
(d) Improved method of cattle-breeding and scientific method of dairying to be introduced.
(e) Different vegetables and fruits should be produced and used by the villagers.
(f) The tools used for agriculture should be gradually improved and manufactured in the villages themselves.

With the rapid advancement in science and technology and innovations of sophisticated textile technology, *Charkha* and Khadi seem to stand a poor chance in the race. The modern technology offers rapid production and competitively cheap cloth. But we should not forget the Gandhian line of thinking. His ecology is also supposed to bring a success, if followed sincerely. About Khadi, Gandhiji says :

> "In reorganising Khadi production you should not forget that the science of Khadi, in some respect, works on diametrically opposite lines to that of ordinary business. You know how Adam Smith in his 'Wealth of Nations' after laying down certain principles according to which the economic phenomena are governed, went on to describe certain other things, which constituted the 'disturbing factor'

> and prevented economic law from having free play, chief among these was the 'human element'. How it is this human element on which the entire economics of Khadi rests and human selfishness, Adam Smith's 'pure economic motive' constitutes the disturbing factor that has got to be overcome."[9]

The Mahatma wanted every home to weave its own yarn. He believed that like cooking every home can weave its own yarn without difficulty.

> "... in spite of every home having its own kitchen, restaurants continue to flourish, so will mills continue to supply our additional wants."[10]

But precaution is always welcome. If we remain alert, we may not suffer. That is to say that even all the mills close anytime, we need not be afraid of that. "Every worker should spin enough for his own requirements. He should be an efficient spinner on the *charkha*, the *dhanush takli* and the *takli*. He should have a thorough knowledge of all the processes prior to spinning—picking, cleaning, ginning, carding, silvering—and spinning. He should know how to mend the wheel and the *dhanush takli* if anything goes wrong with them. All his tools should always be clean and in good order. By his aptness, keenness, intimate knowledge of his work, and personal example he will be able to draw people to Khadi as no amount of propaganda and argument can."[11]

Gandhiji favoured the small-scale industries over the large-scale industries. He did not reject the large-scale industries but he made room for different opinions by the critics. J.C. Kumarappa says, "In the Gandhian system, large-scale mechanised production was rejected because of high social costs."[12] However in the recent years, the economists and the social scientists are considering the impact of mechanical pollution and disturbed ecological balance. So the present shape of the economy itself is proving what he predicted. Gandhiji was right in giving the large-scale industry a secondary place in his system. It creates unemployment, poverty, inequality, concentration of economic power and indulging in heavy social costs. His Khadi and *Charkha* had the right place in the society, which till today is important. One may reject his ideas as impracticable and useless, but the crisis phase through which we are passing reminds us of the utility of his principles. The entire humanity is hanging in danger. Apart from the divergence between marginal social costs and marginal private costs the disturbance in ecological balance too is a serious problem.

Gandhiji was a socialist, though he differed much from other socialists. He was not ready to accept economics as a science of wealth. He even did not accept its role for the enhancement of material gain and happiness. So he differed from Adam Smith to A.C. Pigou or Alfred Marshall. He had similarity with Sismondi in accepting economics as a science of human welfare. But to him welfare was again a subject of moral progress and moral upliftment. So to find a just comparison is as difficult as anything. He did not favour any cut-throat competition in the economy or even the free play of economic doctrines as that of *laissez faire*.

Gandhiji's welfare was for all, so we cannot find a second character in the world to compare with him fully. His ideas and ideals are comparable to only those of great reformers of the world. We know, the great prophets or reformers never find their rightful place in the society easily. They are worshipped and understood after a long time of their expiry even. But it does not imply that they are incorrect in their own times. About Gandhiji too, it holds good. He was precisely what he did for the masses. His politics and economics were intervoven in religion and philosophy. He was so great a character that it is quite impossible for us to draw a correct picture of his personality and worth.

To conclude, it can be said that there was no conflict between his ideas of large-scale or small-scale as such. He just wanted the happiness of the people. And for that he advocated such steps which could fetch the desired results.

His Khadi was not simply a coarse piece of cloth. It was suppressed to liberate the entire human beings in thought and deed both. Many great economists and statesmen miss this underlying interpretation. He was perfectly right in advocating the Khadi in that zeal of those days. It is still practicable and we can still benefit from this. It has not outlived its utility even today. After a very careful thought we can earmark the areas separately for large-scale and small-scale industries. Wherever inevitable in the national interest, items can be reserved for production in large-scale industries. But in order to solve the mounting problem of unemployment, a large number of items can be set apart and earmarked for production in the sphere of Khadi, village and small-scale industries. There is hardly any genuine clash of interest between the two sectors. We have just to strike a fine balance between the two sectors.

It is wrong to presume that there is a constant tug of war between the conflicting claims of large-scale and small-scale industries. There is a vast area of production which can be wisely divided between these two sectors. What is required is a fine reconciliation between the two. Their claims though supposed to be conflicting, have to be understood in proper perspective. And this is what the Mahatma wanted us to realise. The sooner we do it, the better.

REFERENCES

1. *Young India*, dt. 12th October, 1931, p. 318.
2. M.S. Patwardhan, *Modernisation of Indian Industry*, Forum of Free Enterprise, Bombay-1, 14th May, 1986, p. 1.
3. M.K. Gandhi, *Economic and Industrial Life and Relations*, Vol. II, Compiled and edited by V.B. Kher, Navajivan Publishing House, Ist Edn. 1957, p. 33.
4. *Young India*, dt. 9th July, 1919.
5. *Ibid.*, p. 494.
6. *Ibid.*, 13th May, 1919.

7. *M.K. Gandhi*, Navajivan Publishing House, Edn. June 1980, p. 43.
8. *Ibid.*, 25th August, 1920, p. 506 (From : S. Ganeshan's compilation).
9. D.C. Tendulkar, *Mahatma*, Volume III, The Times of India Press, p. 359.
10. *Young India*, From S. Ganeshan's compilation, p. 508.
11. Rajendra Prasad, *Constructive Programme: Some Suggestions*, Navajivan Publishing House, Edn. 1958.
12. J.C. Kumarappa, *Gandhian Economy and Other Essays*.

7

Some Stray Comparisons between Ideas of Gandhi and Marx

Gandhi and Marx, the two giants of modern thinking, have left permanent impression upon us. The two champions of human ideology and great liberators of mankind have brought revolutionary changes in politico-economic thinking of the world.

Though their goal is common—human welfare—their approaches are poles apart. They advocate quite different ways and means to achieve ends. But ends are quite similar. So attention of many is drawn and different explanations are given. An effort to minimise the difference of opinion between these two great personalities has been noticed. In the 20th Congress of C.P.S.U., it was held that violence is not required in socialism. Socialism can be achieved through parliamentary system also. "Ulyañovsky in his essay on Gandhi in his book affirms that Marxists and Leninists were committed to use even the smallest possibilities of peaceful development of the national liberation movement and social revolution and have always considered that from the point of view of the workers and all the working people's real interests peaceful means are preferable to armed struggle."[1]

So efforts have certainly been made to find common points in their views. We can study the main points where they differ and where they do not differ. It is to be studied whether Marxism and Gandhism are complementary to each other or one is 'minus violence' and another is 'plus violence'.

Let us see where the two great immortals agree. Marx wanted expropriation of all private property, that is to say, liquidation of private property. Gandhi also in one sense, agreed to this ideology since he propounded the theory of 'Trusteeship'. In trusteeship too, there is no question of owning one's property individually—things are done collectively and in a co-operative manner. Both realised that this tendency of accumulating wealth will stop exploitation of the poor. 'God has created man after his own image', so, why man should suffer or one should exploit another? This happens in the society when the gap between the two widens. If not tackled in time, it may lead to violent class-conflict and severe chaos. Gandhi did not study Marx. His knowledge on Marx was mostly acquired from talks and discussions. Sometimes he had the opportunity to go through the Marxian ideology sent by some of his Marxist friends. He could see the underlying truth in Marxian ideology. Marx too, he felt, rose above the narrow boundary of class consciousness. He found Marx to be exceedingly favourable to the poor and the exploited. "His diagnosis of the economic malaise may be correct or not", said Gandhiji, "but there is no denying the fact that he thought of doing something for the exploited poor."[2]

Thus we see that they had agreed on a vital issue. In the question of use of machinery, similarity can be traced in both. Marx was well aware of the defects of machines and its other associated evils too. He was of the opinion that man should not become the servant of machines, rather machines should become the servant of man. Marx also held the view that in a machine-age we cannot do without machines. But the point of agreement was that ill-effects of machines should be avoided. About Gandhiji's view on machines, it is at times, held that he was against the use of machines. But Gandhiji has clarified it several times that he was not opposed to the use of machines. To clarify the matter in one line we can quote Gandhiji, "... machines will remain because like the body, they are inevitable."[3] He was just opposed to the craze for machinery. Our life itself is a unique mechanism. But this most complex mechanism of human body responds better to a natural environment. Hence when large-scale use of machines is prescribed the body and nature (i.e. the environment) both react. We are being victimised by the pollution of nature. The very existence of life on this planet has been threatened now. Both Marx and Gandhi realised this truth. However it may be remarked that Gandhiji was for less and less use of machine but Marx never prescribed that machines should be very sparingly used.

About centralisation and decentralisation of industries, the Marxian concept prescribed a planned growth of industries. In it a regional balanced growth has been sought in which maximum gain is to accrue without any violent economic fluctuations. This is very much near the Gandhian ideology and the two ideas can be bracketed together.

Gandhiji was also in favour of nationalisation of industries. In the greater interest of the community he agreed to State control. He remarked :

> "… I am socialist enough to say that such factories should be nationalised, or state-controlled. They ought only to be working under the most attractive and ideal conditions, not for profit, but for the benefit of humanity, love taking the place of greed as motive …The machines will under these conditions, be as much a help to man working it as to the state, or the man who owns it."[4]

Many times Gandhiji has referred himself as a socialist. Yes, he was socialist, and one of the greatest socialists ever born in this world. So his views on nationalisation and state-control are not very different from those of Marx.

About the question of equality and the position of the labour, both Gandhiji and Marx were generous. They wanted the status of labour to be uplifted. Though Gandhiji did not advocate any conflict or violence like that of Marx, but both agreed that social inequality may errupt in violence and bloody revolution. Gandhiji was realist enough to view things before hand. His predictions are true. And so was Marx's. Both wanted to remove the poverty and sufferings of the masses. Both these great personalities were eager to vanish exploitation and misery of the labour or the proletariat.

Now we can try to examine where these two supreme champions of general welfare differ. In the universe, no two perfect things are available or two equal things in nature, shape and size or complexion can be found. Naturally these two great men differ a lot in their theories. Though their goal remained identical, the means to reach the goal were quite contrary. We can discuss and explain some of them.

In a Communist state, production is strictly regulated according to requirements. Consumption and occupation are also as per state directive. It leads to a severe curtailment of individual freedom and liberty. The importance of individual is ignored. But Gandhiji never sacrificed the individual liberty. He considered individual as an indispensable unit of society for all the activities. The very body is the temple of God, he regarded. He was so God-like that he was never ready to sacrifice the interest of individual for the sake of majority. Here Gandhiji is clearly far ahead of Marx. He was really a great champion of individual liberty and freedom.

In Marxism, 'matter' is important, not the 'spirit'. The Marxists do not accept the importance of spirit because for them 'matter' is the ultimate reality. In Gandhiji's principle, spirit has always occupied the superior place. He himself led a pure spiritual life and in words and deeds also maintained balance. So Gandhiji could say, "I do not agree with the view which denies the existence of any entity transcending the physical world. Its existence, however, cannot be proved through the evidence of the senses. It is self-evident. It can be realised only through the inner experience of man. ... In my view the trend of human nature is essentially upward."[5] In Marxism, there is no scope of application of spiritualism.

In the use of machinery, Gandhiji was rather more practical.

His view seems to be much more realistic than others. Marx could not foresee the social, political and economic evils associated with machinery. He was partially aware of the evils of machinery and wanted to be subservient to man. Marx just preferred a systematic use of machinery. Gandhiji was many times more cautious than Marx in the use of machinery. The present age is not only the witness of heavy all-round pollution of machine-age but also the worst sufferer of it.

Love and hatred are two entirely different poles of life. Interestingly, love constituted a vital part of Gandhian ideology. But in Marxian literature, advocacy of hatred of one section of the society by the other is open and above-board. Class-struggle is an example in sight. Louis Fischer expressed that Gandhi was incapable of malice or hatred. Several times in his life the Mahatma demonstrated the power of love and non-retaliation. Some examples can be cited :

(a) A fatal assault by a Pathan in 1908,
(b) The throwing of a bomb-incident at Poona in June 1934,
(c) Attack of hostile Muslim League Members in 1939 at Rajkot,
(d) Attempt of some youth in August 1947 at Calcutta, and
(e) The harassment at Durban in 1896 etc.

But Gandhiji won overall. It was his magic touch of love and non-violence. It was the fundamental difference between Gandhiji and Marx to solve a problem. Gandhiji's most powerful tool was his truth and non-violence. Marx applied the theory of class-struggle and violence to bring the capitalists to book. Gandhiji proved the power of non-violence with amazing success. The English, politically most powerful and economically most advanced and sound, had to withdraw from the soil of India. It was no armed struggle. It was a struggle based on non-violence and non-cooperation. Gandhiji's base of power was his truth to him. So a faith based on truth and non-violence, God and religion was certainly many times more powerful than that of Marx. His non-violent practices were a lesson before the world. The world is on the verge of annihilation. The outburst of the third world-war may finish the human life from this globe. The world fails to realise the inevitable. It is this difference where Gandhiji stands supreme, unsurpassed. The world is bound to listen to his advice someday or the other. The unique theory of non-violence can save the mankind, not violence of the Marxian school. Perhaps this is his greatest contribution to the mankind.

In Marxian literature much importance has been attached to the use of machines. "As soon as tools had been converted from being manual implements of man into implements of a mechanical apparatus, of a machine, the motive mechanism also acquired an independent form, entirely emancipated from the restraints of human strength. Thereupon the individual machine, that we have hitherto been considering, sinks into a mere factor in production by machinery."[6]

The Marxists believe, "... machinery is intended to cheapen commodities, and, by shortening that portion of the working-day, in which the labourer works for himself, to lengthen the other portion that he gives, without an equivalent, to the capitalist."[7] Gandhiji was also in favour of giving the labour a upliftment blended with moral, spiritual, physical progress with a very high standard of plain life. He wanted the progress of human being in all respects. He did not want the machines to play too much a role in the life of human being. What the Marxists took as surplus-value, he did not favour it. For him the human body itself is a unique machine. We can nurture it to the fullest extent.

With regard to choosing means to attain ends, the Marxists have no bar. They can go to any extent. The goal—the end justifies the means. They had the view that any cunning, unlawful method, concealment of truth or evasion can be used for achievement of the cherished goal. They discarded the notion of Democracy. For Gandhiji, a democracy based on obeisance is acceptable. The Marxists had less regard for spiritual and moral values. Human compassions seldom influenced their judgement. Love and pity, truth and non-violence have no place in the Marxian concept. In Marxian paradigm, dictatorship is the only answer to set up a stateless and classless society. However both were against the capitalism and capitalistic structure. "Arguments about the beneficial role of competition are increasingly losing ground among the masses in face of capitalist reality which resembles a pond in which the big fish swallow the small fry with impunity. The domination of the capitalist monopolies in the economy and in all social life has exploded the myth that success in life depends solely on the personal enterprise of the individual. But the more capitalism's contradictions are laid bare, the more hypocritical become the speeches of its apologists."[8]

Thus we see that in spite of nearness between the Gandhian and Marxian concepts, even the gulf of difference is not so shallow. The number of factory workers in the U.S.S.R. has increased much since 1913 which can be shown in the following table :

	1913	*1928*	*1939*	*1959*	*1968*
Entire population (including non-working family members)	100.0	100.0	100.0	100.0	100.0
Factory, Office and other workers.	17.6	17.6	50.2	68.3	77.70
Of whom factory workers	14.0	12.0	32.5	48.2	54.80
Collective farm peasantry and artisans united into co-operatives	—	2.9	47.2	31.4	22.27
Individual peasants and artisans	66.7	74.9	2.6	0.3	0.03
Bourgeoistie, landowners, merchants and kulaks	16.3	4.6	—	—	—

Source : G. Glezerman, *Socialist Society : Scientific Principles of Development*, p. 109.

Thus it is evident that the number if industrial workers in the U.S.S.R. has been increasing. Gandhiji did not like the economy to be engulfed by mechanisation. He wanted the people to be engaged in labour-intensive activities. Simple tools and minimum expenditure in the production process was favoured by him. However he had clarified that large-scale industry is welcome wherever and whenever they are considered relevant on grounds of national interest and requirements.

It is indeed difficult to find out a viable approach to minimise or bridge the gap. At places the difference is so fundamental that they stand like rocks and appear champions of their own concepts.

One of the very basic differences was that Gandhiji was a very much practical, ideal and dynamic personality. Sometimes it appeared that he might be changing his principle or sacrificing one for the sake of another. But it was not so. He was always aware of the time and place factors and could adjust himself accordingly. It is well-known that the Mahatma was a firm believer in non-violence. He would not kill even an insect. So deep was his faith in non-violence. It was his all-pervading love which endeared him to all. But the same Mahatma once agreed to poison a dying calf to help it get rid of unbearable pain. Again, the champion of peace and love and non-violence, had to agree to send a well equipped army to protect Kashmir from Pakistan aggression. Here Gandhiji definitely scores over the champion of communism. Even today Marx is considered to be one of the greatest revolutionary thinkers in the field of politics and economics. His ideas are highly esteemed everywhere. Few advanced nations of the world are following his principles in practice. Though both appeared to be right and appealing in their own ways, the Indian culture makes us akin to Gandhian philosophy. But there is no dearth of countries where Marxian is being practised by States.

To conclude, on this issue, we may just take up one or two issues more to be discussed.

So far both the blocks have claimed their successes and have established their present position in the frame of society. In the Marxian explanation we find that multiplicity of wants is there.

The large-scale industries are there to deliver the goods. But Gandhian economics demonstrated that a society can live happily even by minimisation of wants. Gandhiji went to the extent of clarifying that fulfilment of material wants give short-lived pleasure, not permanent happiness.

Gandhiji's economics was a 'Sarvodaya Economics' or a 'Service Economics', in which our duty is supreme, not our rights. If we follow this dictum, we are to be blessed with permanent happiness. This is indeed a heavenly stage of life. It is the highest order of life one can dream of. However, the socialists believe themselves to be in a 'gregarious' stage of life, where they enjoy perfect harmony. In the gregarious nature of economy, the economic activities are activated to meet the personal and general requirement of life.

About the distribution aspect, the Marxists claim their superiority over the Gandhian set-up. But the distribution process amongst the factors of production is quite arbitrary. There are numerous inside stories of chaos surfacing these days in the communist block of countries. We are aware of these development and feel that Gandhiji's prescription is definitely a better solution. He did not go for much complicated processes and rather efforts are taken to minimise wants in his set-up. So chances of ill-distribution is less. Moreover workers themselves are quite satisfied in their web of small units with minimum wants to fulfil.

About the labour-capital feud, the Gandhian concept stands a better chance to peaceful co-existence. There is virtually no question of infighting because none is in the position to exploit the other or find fault with. Naturally, therefore, we can assert that the concept propounded by Gandhiji if followed, bound to create a better environment in the economic and social sphere.

Thus we have tried to compare these two geniuses of the modern world. It is not justified to place one over another. Both are great indeed. It will require a tremendous and painstaking effort to make a correct assessment of any of them. We cannot dismiss any of the two by a stroke of pen. It is rather felt advisable to conceal that temptation here. Since, points in favour and against are discussed, though in brief, we can at the most hold the view that, Gandhian concept is much more welcome in our Indian context and such other similar economies of the world. This is precisely what we can conclude. We can hope to build a better tomorrow with the help of Gandhiji's tools. But this is our own considered view. Others have every right to differ from us. We may differ to agree with them or agree to differ from them.

REFERENCES

1. Rafiq Zakaria, *Sunday Review — The Times of India*, dt. 30th September, 1984.
2. Chandrashankar Shukla, *Gandhi's View of Life*, 3rd Edn. 1956, Bhartiya Vidya Bhawan, Bombay, p. 3. (quoted from Sushila Nayyar's *Bapu ki Karavas Kahani*), pp. 154, 167.
3. S.S. Gupta, *The Economic Philosophy of Mahatma Gandhi*, Ashok Pub. House, Delhi, p. 185.
4. *Young India*, 13th November, 1924, p. 378.
5. Chandrashankar Shukla, *Gandhi's View of Life*, p. 130.
6. Karl Marx, 'Capital', (A critical analysis of capitalist production) Vol. I, p. 357, Progress Publishers, Moscow, Eng. Edn.
7. *Ibid.*, p. 351.
8. G. Glezerman, *Socialist Society : Scientific Principles of Development*, Progress Publishers, Moscow, First print 1971, p. 205.

8

Conclusion

COMMENTS AND RECOMMENDATIONS

It should be borne in mind that Gandhiji did not acquire his knowledge about India by mere study or hearsay. He travelled length and breadth of the country. He studied the political and economic position of the country and the villages in particular. He did not jump in the national-scene from the heaven. Before joining the Indian political scene he gained enough experience in South Africa. Thus he emerged a champion of non-violence, truth and non-cooperation.

It was his privilege to apply his doctrine in India which was groaning under the pressure of selfish British rule and stark poverty. He lifted the veil of darkness from the nation's eyes. He was able to command the millions in such a natured way that the world was amazed. That was the beauty of his political philosophy. We should not forget that this frail looking giant fought against a most disciplined, advanced nation of the world. He did not raise any hue and cry but silently did what was precisely necessary for the country. That was his mastery of art which he alone could perform.

About the non-violent methods and their application, Gandhiji achieved remarkable success. His, "...principle of Ahimsa or non-violence is as old as the hills but whereas non-violence used to be regarded before as a passive attitude, good only for individuals aspiring to attain spiritual beatitude,

Gandhiji showed how it could be made dynamic and effectively used as a method for the redress of wrongs and establishment of social justice."[1]

He silenced his critics who doubted the usefulness of his methods. He made it such a powerful weapon that the mighty British rule collapsed before the non-violent freedom fighters. In the words of Pyarelal, "Non-cooperation to be successful must mean cooperation amongst all the sections of the community. That calls for the removal of glaring economic inequalities and social injustices that create the gulf between the haves and the havenots, the upperdog and the underdog ; it calls for equal respect for faiths and religions other than one's own, and a broad tolerance in regard to the beliefs and practices of other members of the community."[2]

In his economic thinking too, he used it as one of the most effective measures to fight the ills. However many may prefer violent methods for the attainment of their goal. But the history is there to prove that violence breeds violence. In the words of Jawaharlal Nehru, "Gandhiji found himself unable to give up his fundamental principle of non-violence even in regard to external war. The very nearness of that war became a challenge to him and a test of faith. If he failed at this critical moment either non-violence was not the all-embracing and basic principle and course of action he had believed it to be, or else he was wrong in discarding it or compromising with it. He could not give up the faith of a lifetime on which he had based all his activities, and he felt that he must accept the necessary consequences and implications of that non-violence."[3] Such was his faith from which he never had drifted away. In addition to these, we should remember that ours is a country with rich heritage. The practice of non-violence is one from the time immemorial. The validity of the principle has been proved again and again. Gandhiji was only the latest in the list to do so. So it can be safely held that the principle of non-violence is valid and practicable.

With non-violence, truth is another powerful tool used by Gandhiji. He perfected it to such a degree that he attuned it with

God and God with truth. If one is not true, his non-violence is also a failure. So with non-violence, truth too is of vital importance. Yet he was very practical in his attitude and could adjust situations accordingly. "Gandhi for all his rock-like adherence to certain principles, has shown a great capacity to adapt himself to others and to changing circumstances, to take into consideration the strength and weakness of those others, and especially of the mass of the people, and how far they were capable of acting up to the truth as he saw it."[4] We can prescribe it and trust it for any purpose. A man without truth is of no use to the society. Gandhiji was an embodiment of truth and he applied this for several reasons. He felt that one could sacrifice his very life for the sake of truth. Thus truth holds an important place in Gandhiji's life and politics. It is of course very hard to stick to truth. Since, "What may, therefore, appear as truth to one may appear to be error to another person. And yet both of them may be right, each from his own point of view. Thus Gandhiji early came to the conclusion that pursuit of truth does not admit of violence being inflicted upon one's opponent. Therefore, the doctrine of truth or *Satya*, which Gandhiji described by the word *Satyagraha* or holding on the truth, means vindication of truth by bearing witness to it through self-suffering; in other words, love. *Ahimsa* and Truth are thus the obverse and reverse of the same coin—one is the means, the other the end."[5]

Admittedly Gandhiji has proved that there is place of truth and non-violence even in political life. They can also bring success to political life and practice. These can be blindly recommended to any country, advanced or backward. They can fight political, economic, social, or religious issues by means of truth and non-violence.

Gandhiji's *Satyagraha* movement too is a powerful measure to fight any social, political and economic ills. People do not require to resort to violence. The inner power of *Satyagraha* is splendid. A *Satyagrahi* should be morally very sound. Like non-violence and truth, a *Satyagrahi* is to apply his moral power. Gandhiji had always stressed the moral power to stand against any odds. Also, a *Satyagrahi* must undergo "Courageous, innocent suffering, by purging the emotions of the opponent of anger, fear and pride makes him more receptive to new attitudes and values. Self-purification that accrues to the *Satyagrahi* by his loving self-suffering, on the other hand, enables him to have a more understanding and sympathetic appreciation of the opponent's view point; his weaknesses and redeeming virtues."[6] He attached tremendous importance to moral values of life. He remarked :

> "That, economics is untrue which ignores or disregards moral values. The extension of law of non-violence in the domain of economics means nothing less than the introduction of moral values as a factor to be considered in regulating international commerce."[7] In Satyagraha even a minimum element of violence has no place. "By suffering for truth and justice in his own person cheerfully instead of inflicting suffering upon the opponent the *Satyagrahi* establishes spiritual identity with the opponent and awakens in him the feeling that he cannot hurt him (the *Satyagrahi*) without hurting his own personality."[8] We can view Satyagraha and non-cooperation together. His non-cooperation movement and Satyagraha had completely paralysed the British administration. Seeing the success of Satyagraha and non-cooperation movement we can approve of its use. Non-cooperation is useful in our daily life as well as in the national life. As, "A wife who refuses to part with her ornaments to her drunkard husband and braves his beating, yet never ceases to love and serve him, uses this weapon in its purest form and in the end weans her husband from drink. In the same way, a good citizen will refuse to offer cooperation to Government with a view to weaning it from wrong-doing out of his very desire to cooperate with it consistently with truth and justice. He will, therefore, bear no ill-will or grudge towards the agents of the Government with whom he is non-cooperating. ... His non-cooperation

is but a prelude to cooperation on honourable terms."[9] The Asian countries and other countries too can benefit from it. So about Satyagraha and non-cooperation movement there is little defect. But one should not forget, that these are very hard principles to follow. It requires one to have sound moral courage and power to defend all odds of life. So we are to accept it as a sound policy. One who can adhere to it, is bound to succeed.

Swadeshi is another term in the terminology of Gandhiji. It is the indigenous institutions which keep us going in all walks of our life. If we make ourselves self-sufficient, we are to face the challenge of doing things by our own hands. *Swadeshi* is indeed a precious ideology which gives us courage. The ideology of *Swadeshi* has brought a coherent relationship in economics, politics, religion and philosophy. Gandhiji's *Swadeshi* gave us a new concept of our own state of life. *Swadeshi* movement has added life a new challenge. He could say it boldly, "If crores of people will refuse to wear or use foreign cloth and be satisfied with the simple cloth that we can produce in our homes, it will be proof of our organising ability, energy, cooperation and self-sacrifice that will enable us to secure all we need."[10] But his view was not confined in narrowness. He said, "You will not mistake this for a movement of general boycott of foreign goods. India does not wish to shut herself out of international commerce. Things other than cloth which can be better made outside India, she must gratefully receive upon terms advantageous to the contracting parties. Nothing can be forced upon her."[11] His ideas on *Swadeshi* were very useful in those days. It still holds good and we can recommend the ideology as fit for today even.

So we believe that Gandhiji's political ideas were not at all wrong. We can follow this even today. His closest disciple, Jawaharlal Nehru has rightly observed :

"Gandhi's influence in these various directions has pervaded India and left its mark. But it is not because of his non-violence or economic theories that he has become the foremost and most outstanding of India's leaders. To the vast majority of India's people he is the symbol of India determined to be free, of militant nationalism, of a refusal to submit to arrogant might, of never agreeing to anything involving national dishonour. Though many people in India may disagree with him on a hundred matters, though they may criticize him or even part company from him on some particular issue, at a time of action and struggle when India's freedom is at stake, they flock to him again and look up to him as their inevitable leader."[12]

Any criticism are welcome on it. But so far as experience goes we can say that Gandhiji's political and economic ideas are as sound as any scientific doctrine. These are well-tested ideas of life. There is no fault to be found in these principles which mainly guided his political activities of those days. And he succeeded in his political efforts.

We may take up the issues of Gandhiji's three cardinal concepts also. These cardinal concepts are essential parts of the society. Varna Dharma is the science of hereditary process. There is nothing absurd about it. In the beginning he was really a hard-hitter practitioner of *Varnashramadharma*. But later he became more realistic and accepted inter-marriages also. It is a very good thing to find that Gandhiji at least felt the need to make our life regulated. He should appreciate his ideas on Varnashrama. But by accepting an inter-marriage, he was under criticism. According to him Varna is what one performs. Everybody has got the right to choose his profession. Varna Dharma too is very old—which is continuing on the Indian soil for a long-time. By introducing the Varna Dharma, Gandhiji wanted to create a scientific order of life. He was very clear about his concept on Varna Dharma. We can understand the basic concept from the following :

"Varnashramadharma to my mind is a law which, however

much you and I may deny, cannot be abrogated. To admit the working of that law is to free ourselves for the only pursuit in life for which we are born. *Varnashramadharma* is humility. Whilst I have said that all men and women are born equal, I do not wish therefore to suggest that qualities are not inherited : but on the contrary I believe that just as everyone inherits a particular form so does he inherit the particular characteristics and qualities of his progenitors, and to make this admission is to conserve one's energy. That frank admission, if he will act up to it, would put a legitimate curb upon our material ambitions, and thereby our energy is set free for extending the field of spiritual research and spiritual evolution. It is this doctrine of *Varnashramadharma* which I have always accepted."[13] So we feel that Varna Dharma is acceptable and can be practised.

Gandhiji disliked the idea that in a society one should get exploited by others. Rich do not care for the poor and the poor dies unnoticed. So he advised that the rich should work as a trustee of the society. He felt, "The capitalist, who is found exploiting the people, is made the trustee of the property and so would be expected to use the property, after deducting his maximum permissible income for the public sake."[14] This will stop exploitation of labour. His trusteeship ideology is an improvement over other methods. Gandhiji's ideology is very subtle and practicable. There is no element of violence to be found in Gandhiji's policies and principles. It can eradicate the problem of inequality in the society. We can try this method out and enjoy, a better life in an environment of politically free India. But it is not easy to apply this method, since it involves sacrifice on the part of big farmers. Apart from its drawbacks, the trusteeship principle is a sound policy and can be applied in various conditions. We may hope that this principle is able to solve many other related problems also. This will hold good and can be recommended for any country.

Now we come to the decentralisation policy. In the Indian

context we can apply this method very successfully. Though the decentralisation policy is not accepted in communist countries, India being a land of villages, it is very much necessary to remove the defects of the villages. Gandhiji wanted villages to turn as heaven—fully self-sufficient. So he said :

> "The villagers should develop such a high degree of skill that articles prepared by them should command a ready market outside. When our villages are fully developed there will be no dearth in them of men with a high degree of skill and artistic talent. There will be village poets, village artists, village architects, linguists and research workers. In short there will be nothing in life worth having which will not be had in the villages. Today the villages are dung heaps. Tomorrow they will be like tiny gardens of Eden where dwell highly intelligent folk whom no one can deceive or exploit."[15]

That is why the decentralisation policy is so much applicable and of vast importance to India. Economic conditions of a country will largely determine whether decentralisation is advisable for it. Extent of decentralisation will also differ from country to country.

Gandhiji's view on labour and capital is also unique. He felt the need that labour is never to be exploited. Labour should be free from the bondage of any pressure from any quarters. Labour is the chief source of wealth. Without the active cooperation of labour capital is of no value. It is not capital, but labour which creates or produces. Here Gandhiji attached considerable importance to labour and was eager to give it its rightful place in the process of production. He held that labour is the real owner of the fruits of production. Just as the actual tiller is supposed to be the owner of land, labour is also the owner of the product. However, Gandhiji always advocated for peaceful co-existence of both and in his concept there should not be any conflict between the two. "...conflict arises when one wants to appropriate more than one needs. The greed is at the root of it. With changed outlook and restrictions on greed, the area of conflict will automatically narrow down. Moreover the feelings that the other is not important, and the exaggerated notion about one's own importance also breed conflict. Gandhi, therefore, wanted to make both labour and capital realise that each is ineffective without the other."[16] Since Gandhiji preferred peaceful methods, not the violent methods as advocated in Marxian philosophy, he suggested the rich farmer or owner to be the trustee of the society. He further suggested that we can live together in harmony by cooperative activities. So in view of the above, it can be safely concluded that the circumstances as prevailed in India, his labour theory is definitely an improvement on others. He was a staunch realist too. His powerful visions penetrated deep into the country's problems. He could clearly see the problems and knew their solutions. Hence to dub him an utopian is a gross injustice. He was the champion of the poor and the downtrodden. His remedial measures were sound enough to bring balance in the society. Without much debate we can say that his views on labour and capital are sound and if followed in full can bring an all-round development. We require his ideas to be implemented thoroughly.

In the field of agriculture, Gandhiji suggested a number of ways and means to improve the lot of the peasants. He knew that India lies in her million villages and villages in agriculture. If we cannot supply a handful of rice to the people, our plans and programmes are not of any use. So it is necessary to improve the condition of land and introduce cooperative farming in the villages. "Cooperative farming of his conception would change the face of the land and banish poverty and idleness from their midst. All this was only possible if people became friends of one another and as one family. When that happy event book place there would be no ugly sore in the form of a communal problem."[17] He devised very simple mechanism to combat the ills related to agrarian problems. His suggestions, though simple are perhaps free in nature are full of promises. About preparation of compost, supply of water in the fields, cooperative activities, etc. Gandhiji has gone into details. We find no objection to them. It is rather very much useful for us. The country is facing a serious problem of unemployment. But if we can absorb the people in occupations as shown by Gandhiji, this is certain to bring success. Apart from this, his various tips on our food-habits too are important. He suggested, "If we would be national instead of provincial, we should have to have an interchange of habits as to food, simplify our tastes and produce healthy dishes all can take with impunity. This means a careful study of the foods taken by different provinces, castes and denominations. Unfortunately, or fortunately, there are not only different combinations in different provinces, but there are different styles in the same province, among the different communities. It is necessary, therefore, for national workers to study the foods and the methods of preparing them in the various provinces and discover common, simple and cheap dishes which all can take without upsetting the digestive apparatus."[18] We can obviously maintain sound health, if we follow his advice. His suggestions to improve the agriculture are so unique that the fields too will never lose their fertility. He did not favour the use of chemical fertilizer which ultimately rob the fields of its fertility power. Every year we sacrifice millions of rupees in foreign exchange for payment of imports. These are not necessary. But it is observed that Gandhian techniques seem simple and operative, but is practically not so. It is indeed very difficult to bring a change in agriculture on his lines. But we cannot say at this stage even that the Mahatma was wrong. He was never wrong in his approach. Rather we lack the required zeal to put his theory into practice. If our Government feels the need to revive our agriculture and villages in the Gandhian way, this can be achieved. His theory of trusteeship and cooperative farming are quite feasible and hence can safely be recommended.

The controversy between the large *versus* small-scale industries relating to use of machines is a matter of one's outlook and ability to look into the impending problems. He was right enough to prescribe the small-scale and cottage industries in lieu of large-scale industries. He was aware of the vicious problems related to the large-scale industries. He has rightly observed, "The workers in the mills of Bombay have become slaves. The condition of the women working in the mills is shocking. When there were no mills, these women were not starving. If the machinery craze grows in our country, it will become an unhappy land. It may be considered a heresy, but I am bound to say that it were better for us to send money to Manchester and to use flimsy Manchester cloth than to multiply mills in India. By using Manchester cloth we only waste our money; but by reproducing Manchester in India, we shall keep our money at the price of our blood, because our very moral being will be sapped, and I call in support of my statement the very mill-hands as witnesses. And those who have amassed wealth out of factories are not likely to be better than other rich men."[19] The large-scale industries not only create unemployment, but become a health-hazard in the surroundings. Money too accumulate in the few pockets. However Gandhiji has clarified it nicely that he did not oppose the use of machineries or large-scale industries so far these are concerned with pure human welfare. If people are rendered unemployed due to large factories, if labour is exploited and moral values are degraded, Gandhiji was dead against such industries. He was purely in favour of use of only those machineries which serve human being like anything. If the very purpose of human welfare is defeated, Gandhiji was seriously rigid there. He observed, "The heavy machinery for the work of public utility which can be undertaken by human labour has its inevitable place but all that would be owned by the state and used entirely for the benefit of the people."[20]

We can easily derive from this that he was aware of the defects of private ownerships of large-scale industries. Therefore, he did not want to give the chance to private owners to exploit the labour. He sealed that chance by preferring it in favour of State ownership. Such industries are to be only few those key industries which are essential and unavoidable. We must conclude that Gandhiji was realistic enough to point out the defects which are surfacing these days. Apart from the unemployment, heavy capital requirement etc., the large-scale sophisticated industries are now a threat to the existence of very human life. Steps are being devised all-over the world to fight environment and water pollutions, etc. Now, without hesitation we can come to the conclusion that Gandhiji was very much right to prefer the small over the big. Small is beautiful. When we confront population and unemployment problems, we have to accept Gandhiji in heart and soul. In Indian circumstances his theory is true to the letters.

About Khadi and similar village-industries, Gandhiji again stands as a champion of the cause of Indian economy. If we try to view the ideology of *Charkha* and Khadi, it is a beauty in itself. The power of that simple spinning wheel is so tremendous that it can completely and successfully unite the whole country from Kashmir to Kanyakumari. It is a simple but most powerful device to give the people moral and economic strength and a feeling of self-reliance. He says, "The spinning wheel represents to me the hope of the masses. The masses lost their freedom, such as it was, with the loss of the *Charkha*. The *Charkha* supplemented the agriculture of the villagers and gave it dignity. It was the friend and solace of the widow. It keeps the villagers from idleness. For the *Charkha* included all the anterior and posterior industries—ginning, carding, warping, sizing, dyeing and weaving. These in their turn kept the village carpenter and the blacksmith busy. The Charkha enabled the seven hundred thousand villages to become self-contained. With the exit of the Charkha went the other village industries, such as the oil press. Nothing took the place of these industries. Therefore, the villages were drained of their varied occupations and their creative talent and what little wealth these brought them.

"Hence, if the villagers are to come into their own, the most natural thing that suggests itself is the revival of the Charkha and all it means."[21] His ideas are not to be taken as disjointed precepts—these are with the goal of 'goodness of human nature', as a whole. He emerged as the sole champion of 'growth for justice'. Now all of us are never tired of repeating the slogan of 'growth for justice'.

The champion of Gandhian ideology Vinoba Bhave observed:

> "...though the Gandhian ideology stands nowhere in an organised form, yet inasmuch as it is impregnated with the virility of right thinking. I believe that ultimately it will be Gandhism with which communism will have its trial of strength."[22]

So days are not far, when the entire world will have to seek peace in Gandhism. The mass in general wants peace and non-violence in life. Love is the key to happiness. To make the life spiritually healthy and morally sound, we must spread the message of human love. Economic wealth is of no importance to us, it is devoid of human affection. In the words of another Mahatma, Thakur Anukul Chandra :

> "Where sufferance for the Love
> is a blessing,
> where hearth and home
> are satisfied,
> blended with sweet relation,
> economic wealth of the country
> normally flows
> in a puffing flow."[23]

So we feel, it is indeed a very difficult task to clarify the Mahatma as he was. His many sided talents and godly qualities are so high and deep that it is very difficult to equate or compare him with anybody.

About Marx and Gandhiji, we can say that both are two pillars of human welfare. Since Gandhiji advocated peaceful means of non-violent nature and sanctioned complete freedom of thought, speech and action, he has an edge over Marx. Gandhiji remained a bit more liberal and flexible than his counterpart. But both were against the evils of capitalism. "Contemporary capitalism provides more and more evidence that Marx was right. Mankind has now entered the era of another scientific and technological revolution linked with the automation of production, the harnessing of nuclear energy, space exploration and so on. But capitalism seeks to turn all these greatest attainments of the human mind against mankind itself. Harnessed nuclear energy, which promises people unlimited sources of cheap industrial power, has been converted by imperialism into the threat of a lethal devastating war."[24] However, it will be sheer disgrace to place the importance of one over another. We can safely leave it in the hands of future to pronounce its judgement. But in the Indian context, Gandhiji was definitely a supreme commander of things where none can excel him.

Pandit Jawaharlal Nehru who had deep regard for Gandhiji has remarked :

> "Gandhiji knew India and especially the Indian masses, as very few, if any, have known them in the past or the present. Not only had he widely travelled all over India and come into touch with millions of people, but there was something else which enabled him to come into emotional contact with those masses. He could merge himself with the masses and feel with them, and because they were conscious of this, they gave him their devotion and loyalty."[25]

So on the basis of critical assessment we come to the conclusion that in India and in her present day problems, the solution lies in relying upon Gandhian model. Wilfred Wellock has remarked in a very convincing manner :

> "Some indication of the revolution that is needed may be witnessed in India, where an attempt is being made to erect a

> civilisation on principles which at every stage insure the culture of the whole man. The conditions by which the most cultural and capable human beings and the happiest societies may be produced are believed to exist in the Gandhian concept of Village Republics. In the villages of India, Gandhian constructive workers are today trying to produce better patterns of human living and human association than those which have brought the West to its present pass. And so great is their faith that they are working on a substance basis."[26]

Now the real judge is time. Unless his ideologies are tested practically in full we cannot negotiate their importance and suitability. It is urged that statesmen give a trial, a fair trial, to Gandhian thoughts and ideology. If it is not possible to inject his thought from the grassroots to the top, we cannot hope a better deal. Half-hearted measures seldom succeed. So it is hoped that Gandhian thought and ideology will prove its mettle in the coming days ahead. As yet we have not given a fair trial, not even a trial to Gandhian economic ideology. Though we are never tired of repeating that Gandhiji and his ideology are still suited to our economic conditions to a very large extent, we have not sincerely tried to implement his economic ideas. 'It is never too late to mend', goes the wise saying.

REFERENCES

1. Pyarelal, *Gandhian Techniques in the Modern World*, Navajivan Publishing House, Edn. November, 1969, p. 11.
2. *Ibid.*, p. 13.
3. Jawaharlal Nehru, *The Discovery of India*, The Signet Press, Calcutta, Ist End. 1946, p. 535.
4. *Ibid.*, p. 538.
5. Pyarelal, *Gandhian Techniques in the Modern World*, Navajivan Publishing House, Edn. November, 1969, p. 7.
6. *Ibid.*, p. 9.
7. *Young India*, dt. 10th May, 1928, p. 145.

8. Pyarelal, *Gandhian Techniques in the Modern World*, Navajivan Publishing House, Edn. November, 1969, p. 10.
9. *Ibid.*, pp. 12-13.
10. M.K. Gandhi, *Young India*, Aug. 25, 1920. (S. Ganesan's compilation), p. 506.
11. *Young India*, Aug. 25, 1920, p. 506.
12. Jawaharlal Nehru, *Discovery of India*, p. 539.
13. M.K. Gandhi, *Varnashramadharma*, Navajivan Publishing House, Edn. 1962, pp. 24-25.
14. S.S. Gupta, *The Economic Philosophy of Mahatma Gandhi*, Ashok Publishing House, Delhi-32, p. 95.
15. M.K. Gandhi, *Village Industries*, Navajivan Publishing House, Ist Edn. 1960, pp. 18-19.
16. S.S. Gupta, *The Economic Philosophy of Mahatma Gandhi*, Ashok Publishing House, Delhi, pp. 123-24.
17. M.K. Gandhi, *India's Food Problem*, Navajivan Publishing House, Ahmedabad, Ist. Edn. 1960, p. 21.
18. *Ibid.*, p. 52.
19. M.K. Gandhi, *Hind Swaraj or Indian Home Rule*, Navajivan Publishing House, Ahmedabad, Reprint 1982, p. 94.
20. M.K. Gandhi, *Economic and Industrial Life and Relations*, (Vol. II). Ed. By V.B. Kher, Navajivan Publishing House, Jan. 1967. (Quoted from *Harijan*, June 22, 1935, p. 147), pp. 47-48.
21. M.K. Gandhi, *Panchayat Raj*, Navajivan Publishing House, 2nd Edn. Nov., 1969, p. 25.
22. S.S. Gupta, *The Economic Philosophy of Mahatma Gandhi*, (quoted from 'Gandhi and Marx' — by K.G. Mashruwala, p. 15), p. 192.
23. Sri Sri Thakur Anukul Chandra Chakraborty, *The Message*, Vol. VIII, Satsang Pub. House, Deoghar, 2nd Edn. 1983, p. 342.
24. G. Glezerman, *Socialist Society : Scientific Principles of Development*, Progress Pub., Moscow, Ist Printing 1971, p. 248.
25. Pandit Jawaharlal Nehru, *The Discovery of India*, The Signet Press, Calcutta, Ist Edn. 1946, p. 546.
26. Wilfred Wellock, *'New Horizons' Build the Future Now*, Pub. Housemans' Bookshop, London, N.4, p. 6.

Bibliography

Works of Gandhiji

An Autobiography.
All Men are Brothers.
Basic Education.
Birth Control—The Right Way and the Wrong Way.
Cent Per Cent Swadeshi or *The Economics of Village-Industries.*
Co-operative Farming.
Diet and Diet Reform
Economic and Industrial Life and Relations. Vols. I-III (Compiled & Edited by V.B. Kher, 1957)
Economics of Khadi.
Ethical Religion.
Food Shortage and Agriculture.
From Yervada Mandir.
Gandhiji Expects (Compiled by H.M. Vyas).
Harijan.
Hind Swaraj or *Indian Home Rule.*
Hindu Dharma.
India of My Dreams.
India's Food Problem.
Khadi (Hand-spun cloth)— Why and How.
My Socialism.
My Non-violence.
Non-violent Way to World Peace.
Non-violence in Peace and War— Vol. I
Non-violence in Peace and War— Vol. II

Panchayat Raj.
Prohibition at Any Cost.
Rebuilding our Villages.
Sarvodaya.
Satyagraha : Non-violent Resistance.
Self-restraint vs *Self-indulgence.*
Strikes.
Satyagraha in South Africa.
Selections from Gandhi (Edited by Sri N.K. Bose, Navajiṿan Pub.)
The Moral Basis of Vegetarianism.
Truth Called them Differently.
The Gospel of Renunciation.
The Collected Works of Mahatma Gandhi—Vol. I to V. (Published by Publications Division of India).
Trusteeship.
Varnashramadharma.
Village Industries.
Voluntary Poverty.
Why Khadi and Village Industries (Edited by V. Kothari, Published by Navajivan Pub.).
Women.
Young India, 1919-22, (Ganesan's Compilation, 1923).
Young India, 1924-26, (Ganesan's Compilation, 1927).
Young India, 1927-28, (Ganesan's Compilation, 1935).

Works of others

Alexander, Horace & others, *Social and Political Ideas of Mahatma Gandhi,* Indian Council of World Affairs, New Delhi.
Agarwal, A.N., *Gandhism, A Socialistic Approach,* Ahmedabad.
Andrew, C.F., *Mahatma Gandhi's Ideas,* London.
Bilpodiwala, Noshir, *The Social Order and Sarvodaya,* (Pub. Sarva Seva Sangha, Varanasi).
Bose, R.N., *Gandhian Technique & Tradition,* (Research Division, All India Institute of Social Welfare & Business Management, Calcutta).

Choudhary, R., *Bapu As I Saw Him,* (Navajivan Pub.).
Cole, G.D.H., *What Marx Really Meant,* London.
Collins, Larry & Dominique Lapierre, *Freedom At Midnight,* (Vikas Publishing House).
Dantwala, M.L., *Gandhism Reconsidered*, (Padma Publications, Bombay).
Dhawan, G.N., *The Political Philosophy of Mahatma Gandhi*, (Navajivan Pub.).
Diwakar, R.R., *Satyagraha in Action*, (Signet Press, Calcutta).
Diwakar, R.R., *Satyagraha*, (Hind Kitab, Bombay).
Desai, Mahadev, *Gandhiji in Indian Villages,* Madras.
Dutta, Bhabotosh, *Indian Economic Thought*, (McGraw-Hills, New Delhi).
Desai Mahadev, *How does Mahatma Gandhi Live at Sewashram.*
Fisher, Louis, *Gandhi,* Delhi.
Gide & Rist, *History of Economic Thought.*
Glezerman, G., *Socialist Society : Scientific Principles of Development.* (Pub. by Progress Publishers, Moscow).
Gregg, R.B., *Economics of Khaddar*, (Navajivan Pub.).
Gregg, R.B., *A Discipline for Non-violence*, (Navajivan Pub.).
Gregg, R.B., *Power and Non-violence*, (Navajivan Pub.).
Gupta, (Dr.) S.S., *Economic Philosophy of Mahatma Gandhi.*
Gandhi, Manubahen, *The End of an Epoch.*
Jain, Jawahirlal, *Sarvodaya Arthavyavastha* (Hindi), (Bhartiya Granthmala, Allahabad).
Kripalani, J.B., *Gandhi—A Political Study,* (Sarva Sewa Sangha, Wardha).
Kripalani, J.B., *The Gandhian Way,* Bombay.
Kumarappa, Bharatan, *Capitalism, Socialism & Villagism,* Madras.
Kumarappa, J.C., *Economy of Permanence,* Vols. I & II, (The All India Village Industries Association, Wardha).
Kumarappa, J.C., *Gandhian Economy and other Essays.*
Khosla, K.R., *Mahatma Gandhi, Life Through Pictures.*
Mashruwala, K.G., *Political Non-violence*, (Navajivan).
Mashruwala, K.G., *Gandhi and Marx*, (Navajivan).
Munshi, K.M., *Gandhi's View of Life*, (Bhartiya Vidya Bhawan).

Mehta, J.K., *Advanced Economic Theory*.

Marx, K., *Capital*, (Progress Publishers, Moscow) Vol. I.

Mehta, Ashoka, *Socialism & Gandhism*, Bombay.

Nehru, Jawaharlal, *The Discovery of India*, (The Signet Press, Calcutta).

Prabhu, R.K., *This was Bapu*, (Navajivan).

Patwardhan, M.S., *Modernisation of Indian Industry*, (Forum of Free Enterprises, Bombay).

Prasad Rajendra, *Satyagraha in Champaran*, (Navajivan).

Prasad Rajendra, *Constructive Programme—Some Suggestions*, (Navajivan).

Pyarelal, *Gandhian Technique in the Modern World*.

Ruskin, *Unto the Last*.

Ronald Duncan, *The Writings of Gandhi*, (University Press, Oxford).

Singh, V.B., *From Naoroji to Nehru*, (Navajivan).

Shukla, Chandrashankar, *Gandhi's View of Life*, (Bhartiya Vidya Bhawan).

Shah, Ghanshyam & Chaturvadi, H.R., *Gandhian Approach to Rural Development*, (Ajanta Publications, Delhi).

Tendulkar, D.G., *Mahatma*, Vols. I-VIII, (The Times of India Press).

Thakur, Anukul Chandra, *'The Message'*, Vol. VIII.

Thakur, Anukul Chandra, *'The Message'*, Vol. IX.

Vinogradov, V., *Socialist Nationalisation of Industries*, (Progress Publishers, Moscow).

Wellock, Willfred, *New Horizons, Build The Future Now*, (Houseman's Bookshop, London, N.-4).

Papers and Magazines

Amrit Bazar Patrika,
Hindustan Standard,
Times of India,
The Indian Express,
The Yojana.

Index